Last century, there were three great Presbyterian Churches, in Scotland, all of them nation-wide. One, the United Presbyterian Church has vanished, having merged with the Free Church in 1900 to form the United Free Church. Of the Disruption Free Church, sections are to be found in five denominations – the United Free Church, the Free Church, the Church of Scotland, (by union with the U.F. Church in 1929), the Free Presbyterian Church, and the Associated Presbyterian Churches.

The latest division, that of the Associated Presbyterian Churches from the Free Presbyterian Church, took place in 1989. The author finds the question of liberty of conscience, which is a direct consequence of the open door between heaven and earth, over which the division took place going back to the origins of the Free Presbyterian Church. A side issue is the question of the rightful possessor of the property. This was a matter of practical concern to him, since he stayed in one of the manses which were taken over by the Free Presbyterian Church. The cause of the emergence of two streams from the Disruption Free Church in 1893 (the Free Presbyterian Church) and 1900 (the Free Church) are explored, in particular from the standpoint of liberty of conscience.

The most fundamental concern for all churches of a conservative bent, in the view of the author, is the present-day secular humanism which has taken over the soul of our country. The author has touched on the emergence of this. The highlighting of the issues relating to liberty of conscience is aimed at a resolution of divisions by exploring the relation of liberty of conscience to the emergence of each.

The author is a minister of the Associated Presbyterian Churches staying in Thurso and serving churches in Wick, Thurso and Strathy.

Cover Picture: from a painting by Cathol Morrison.

THE OPEN DOOR

S. Fraser Tallach.

Published by Weydale Publishing.

March, 1996.

Further copies may be obtained from:

Rev. S. Fraser Tallach,
"Morven",
Duncanshill,
THURSO.
KW14 8YN.

ISBN   0 9526686 0 2

CONTENTS

PART I; LESSONS OF HISTORY

CHAPTER 1

TO WHOM IT MAY BELONG

The building on the cover of this book is a manse.

Manses come in a whole variety of forms. There are huge, solid buildings that might be mistaken for castles if they had towers at their corners. This one is of the more modern type, a sensible two storied house which lacks the mystique of older buildings, but compensates in terms of ease of use - no high ceilings to which heat may rise while ground level remains like an ice-box, no garrets where mice or rats may lurk.

What sets a manse apart is not its style but its use. It is the house of a minister - a minister of the Word of God. It is a house provided by a community for this minister. The community in question in this case was the community of Free Presbyterians in this corner of Scotland to which I came in 1980.

Being a community house, a manse should have an open door into the community. The first minister who made a deep impact on this North-West corner of Scotland was an Alexander Munro. He found a closed door when he came, and had to forge an open door for himself. The people he found largely ignorant of the Bible but abounding in tunes and poetry. He translated the Bible into rhyme. He then had the people memorise Scripture truth and sing it to the tunes with which they were familiar.

Equally, there should be an open door from the community into the manse. The importance of that open door was impressed on me shortly after I came. On a Saturday night when I was trying to hammer into shape my two sermons for the next day, a knock came to the back door. When I opened it, two figures stood between the glow of the light from the hall-way, and the darkness beyond. They stood there silent, but evidently waiting to be asked in.

I knew neither of them. My mind went through several somersaults in trying to frame an appropriate response. It seemed unlikely there was a spiritual motive in their visit. If they were coming for a chat, might there not be plenty of future opportunities. I explained this was not the most convenient of times and could they visit again? With that I closed the door.

One of these men was Derek Morrison from Manse Road. The other was Alasdair Tom. Not long after I saw Derek at the garage, and slipped into the front seat of his car. I had quite a long talk with him which I thought might have been the precursor of many more. It was not to be. Shortly thereafter, while moving his boat from the Loch Clash harbour to the Loch Bervie harbour, Derek was drowned in heavy seas while rounding the headland. His body was never found.

For the most part, the door was open. It was open to James McRory when he came to show me photos of how his house, away out in the hills, had been done up and to find out my birthday so that he could tell me my fortune. When I tried to turn the tables and meet his occult views with some solid theology I was invariably ineffective. He had worked out New Testament Christianity according to the signs of the Zodiac individuals in New Testament history had been born under, and that was enough for him. It was open for Malcolm and Chirsty when they came to play marbles, usually with more or less of a retinue of other children from the district. (When I first drew a circle in chalk in the carpet as a target for the marbles, Malcolm stood over me and asked solemnly, as a grandparent might gently question the first erring steps of youth, "Does your house-keeper know that you do this?") It was open during the week for Bible Studies and at the week-end for Sabbath School. It was open at communion times for visiting ministers and others who came for the season.

Principally, it is in neither of these "horizontal" senses of an open door, either from the manse into the district or from the district to the manse that I have used the phrase in the title.

A minister comes as a herald. He comes because God has opened a door to Him so that he may teach others "with the Holy Ghost sent down from heaven." It was in this way the door was opened to Alexander Munro. Robert Bruce, the Edinburgh minister, had been exiled to Inverness. Under his preaching, Alexander Munro was converted. Shortly after this experience, he heard a call, though in what precise form we cannot now say, to the far-flung parish of Durness which stretched from Tongue to Eddrachillis. "At his entry", says the account of his ministry in the "Fasti", "the people are stated to have been almost heathen, but his labours met with much success."

The last series of Bible Studies in the manse was on the Seven Churches of Asia in Revelation. One of these studies, the one on the Church in Philadelphia, brought back memories. Philadelphia was a church that had " a little strength" but had not denied Christ's name, and to her was given the unique promise by Christ, "I have set before thee an open door, and no man can shut it." When I was in Broadford, my previous charge, I had received a call to Kinlochbervie. I had given some encouragement that the call go on, but in a moment of uncertainty phoned Rev. D. B. Macleod, who was to preach the induction sermon, to say that I had certain qualms. "I already have the induction sermon prepared." said Mr Macleod, "I will be preaching on 'I have set before thee an open door and no man can shut it.' "

The induction went ahead.

In 1989 came the split between the Free Presbyterian Church and the Associated Presbyterian Churches. I took the side of the Associated Presbyterian Churches, and remained in the manse. For worship we had to find alternative accommodation since the two churches in Scourie and Kinlochbervie remained with the Free Presbyterians.

The split is a sad affair, as every split between Christians is. Last century, the Higlands were all but unified under the 1843 Free Church. So united were they that at one point Dr Kennedy led a movement to have the Free Church declared the established church in the Highland area rather then the Church of Scotland. It was the south of Scotland that had its splits. Now the splits in the south are all but gone, the two other main denominations there - United Presbyterian and Free Church - being all but absorbed in the Church of Scotland. A hundred years later, in the Highlands, four Presbyterian bodies share the ground. There is the Church of Scotland, the Free Church, the Free Presbyterian and the Associated Presbyterian Churches.

"How do you justify your position?" asked a Free Church minister when I was on a visit to the Isle of Skye this summer. On the same visit, in semi-jocular vein, a Free Presbyterian minister said. "When are you prodigal sons going to return to the fold? The Free Presbyterian Church welcomes prodigals." Tensions have been heightened by the taking over of manses, among them my old manse, by force. I feel I am doing no more than a service if I set out in a logical way the claim of the

Associated Presbyterian Churches to be in direct continuity, so far as the particular witness she has contended for, not only with the original stance of the Free Presbyterian Church at its outset, but with the distinctive stance of the Scottish Reformed Church. I do this, not to make division more entrenched, but to make any dialogue which may take place more intelligent.

That distinctive witness has been on the subject of liberty of conscience. I will translate that into the open door, both in its verticle and its horizontal axes. The vertical axis involves the headship of Christ over the Church, the gift of his Spirit to her so that she may know God's good and acceptable and perfect will, and the return by the Church of sacrifices of prayer, praise and service. These categories involve Christian liberty and the priesthood of all believers. The horizontal axis, viz. that which concerns the duty of the Church here on earth, involves the right to rebut any attempt to coerce the conscience of the believer in the performance of his duty by ensnaring it in requirements to give either implicit faith or blind obedience to commands which are contrary to the Word of God or beside it.

My route in this vindication will be rather circuitous. It will be through Scripture, the Reformation, and the section of the Church of Scotland which developed the principles which came to expression in the Disruption. I remember a story as a child which told of two yachts which were in process of racing each other. The skipper of one spied a ruffle of wind far off in the open sea. He made for it, though in doing so he was travelling at a wide angle from the finishing line and was adding considerably to the distance he covered. Once he reached the breeze, his sails filled and he sped to the finishing line well in advance of his rival. I hope to emulate him.

First, I will explain more fully the reason for my journey.

PART 1: LESSONS OF HISTORY

CHAPTER 2

THE TWO CENTENARIES

In 1996 we are now roughly half way between the centenary of the separation of the Free Presbyterian Church from the (1843) Free Church of last century and the separation of the present-day Free Church from the same body in 1900. The celebrations of the Free Presbyterian Church in 1993 have moved into the past. These consisted, notably, in a meeting of representatives from various areas of the world in the hall where the Assembly of the Church of Scotland at present meets, and before the very table on which Mr Macfarlane, the main originator of the Free Presbyterian Church, laid his protest. There was also the publication of a centenary volume. At the end of the century, the (1900) Free Church will have their celebrations.

The heat of·battle which marked the early years of this century between the two churches has largely cooled. The claim is made on any suitable occasion by one or the other that that particular body represents the true Reformed Church of the Reformation, but, whether it is because each has established its own position, or it is felt that such discussions at this late date would be pointless, the very areas of disagreement which led to the two churches emerging as separate bodies have been largely forgotten.

So far as ceasing to jostle for position in a spirit of rivalry is concerned, that is no bad thing. So far as sinking into a spirit of inertia and failing to confront the issues at stake, it cannot but be harmful. Particularly at a centenary, there should be a mature attempt to question why the separation of two bodies so close to one another in worship and doctrine happened in the first place.

First, it is best to unravel the situation of the various churches concerned. The mid-point of last century saw three main Presbyterian bodies share the allegiance of the Presbyterian faithful in Scotland. There was the Church of Scotland, the Free Church of Scotland which had separated from the parent body in 1843, and the United Presbyterian Church which was formed by a fusion of the United Secession Church and the Relief Church three years before the half-century. The momentum towards union brought the Free Church and the United Presbyterian Church into one in 1900. For some in the Highlands the F.C. Declaratory Act (1892) which was clearly aimed at expediting the union was too much to bear. The result was a split in 1893 and a further split in 1900.

When both churches parted from the same parent body over the passing of the same Act, why the distance in time between the separation of the Free Presbyterian Church, which came out in 1893 at the time the Act was passed, and the (1900) Free Church which carried on the name of the (1843) Free Church into the twentieth century after the main bulk of the (1843) Free Church had united with the United Presbyterian to become the United Free Church? Prior to 1893, the personnel which made up the Free Presbyterian Church and those who later came out with the Free Church were united in a common cause within the Free Church somewhat in the same way as the anti-Europeans in the Conservative Party are united to secure that integration into Europe is not carried beyond a certain extent. Their scruples make them a distinct pressure group though not to the extent of separation from the Party. For the Constitutional Party, the crunch came in 1892. The doctrinal constitution for the Constitutional Party was the Confession of Faith. All within the

Constitutional Party agreed that the Declaratory Act passed in the Assembly that year, sold the Confession down the river. Why was there not a united separation at that time?

The answer is as follows. The terms of the relevant question put to office-bearers on their ordination both before and after the passing of the Declaratory Act were, "Do you sincerely own and believe the whole doctrine contained in the Confession of Faith, approven by former General Assemblies of this Church, to be founded upon the word of God?" The question over which the two churches, Free Presbyterian and Free Church, divided was whether this question allowed the Declaratory Act to come into operation or not, or whether those seeking relief under the Act would have to wait till the questions were clearly brought into alignment with the Declaratory Act. The Free Presbyterian Church claimed that without more ado the Declaratory Act modified the whole doctrine contained in the Confession of Faith. An Act passed in 1894 saying that any office-bearer desiring relief under the Act could take his vows "in view of the Declaratory Act" confirmed their stance. Any minister who was part of a presbytery ordaining a probationer who answered that question in the affirmative, was bound to be administering the Declaratory Act. That such active complicity in the operation of the Declaratory Act was impossible without the surrender of vital principle was the commonly agreed opinion of all within the Constitutional Party. The only answer was separation.

The reply of the (1900) Free Church in exoneration of their delay in separating was that the Questions and Formula which brought the Act into operation in the ordination of office-bearers were not actually changed, and in view of the intentions to change the Questions and Formula to bring them into line with the changed doctrinal stance of the Church, it was premature to separate until these changes were made. The changes were finally introduced directly prior to the union of United Presbyterian Church and Free Church in 1900. The view of the minority in the Free

Church which eventually became the present Free Church at that time was, "The said *adjustment of the Questions and Formula to be subscribed by the ministers and elders of the so-called United Free Church of Scotland imported an abandonment by the Unionist members of the Free Church of the Westminster Confession,* and therefore an abandonment of the constitutional standard of their Church's belief." ("Free Church Appeals", p. 37). Since the Free Presbyterian Church separated before there was any real necessity to do so, they acted schismatically. In doing so, in their opinion, they acted in contravention of their ordination vows which required them to "maintain the unity and peace of this church against error and schism, notwithstanding of whatsoever trouble or persecution may arise."

Such a relatively simple and technical difference of opinion would be so overshadowed, surely, by the gravity of the real doctrinal issues at stake, on which both sides were agreed, that, for all the initial division, the union of the two churches could not long be delayed. At this point a curious quirk makes its appearance and this quirk means that a straightforward setting out of the respective cases of the two churches, as has been attempted above, may represent truth, but not the whole truth and nothing but the truth. The Free Presbyterian Church did not separate till 1893. The Declaratory Act was passed in 1892. What caused the delay?

Whatever that cause might have been, the Free Church would claim the Free Presbyterian Church acted schismatically on two fronts. They did so in relation to the main body of the Free Church in separating before the Declaratory Act was really imposed on the Church as a whole. In relation to those with whom they had common cause till 1892 when the Declaratory Act was passed, i.e. the rest of the minority who carried on to become the Free Church of 1900, they acted schismatically also. The Free Presbyterian Church, argue the Free Church, were just as much under the Declaratory Act between 1892 and 1893 as the Free Church were between 1892 and 1900. The point is made by Prof. J. Kennedy Cameron in a letter to "The Northern Chronicle" in July, 1923. Mr Macfarlane replied that he was under protest that year. Prof. Cameron replied that the minority which continued on to 1900 entered the same protests, and should have been protected too.

> "One year's guilt, if guilt there be, effectively compromises a party as well as that of several years. I have endeavoured to show in my book referred to that the 1894 Act of the Free Church Assembly states that the Declaratory Act was merely declarative. The minority asserted that the passing of it was 'ultra vires', and the civil courts established their contention. Their continuance in the Church was accordingly justified, and saved them from the schism in which otherwise they would have been involved."

> "What he, (Mr Macfarlane), maintains, however, is that his protests and statements protected him from complicity in the wrong-doing of the Church in passing such legislation. If this was so in his case, were not the dissents and protests of the minority who remained in the Church equally valid in protecting them?"

Hence, the (1900) Free Church would claim, the Free Presbyterian Church is involved in a kind of double schism. When ministers separated in 1893 after staying on a whole year post-1892 under the same conditions as the ministers who separated in 1900, they acted schismatically and contrary to the earlier claims made by them that their protest gave them protection from the Act. There is no logical reason, it is claimed, why their brotherly union with the other Constitutional ministers could not have been maintained till 1900 when they would have become ministers in the present Free Church.

Real benefit can come from any revival of interest in either 1893 or 1900, only if there is a determined effort to reassess the whole situation. (In such a reassessment, the Associated Presbyterian Churches and Free Presbyterian Church challenge the (1900) Free Church as one, simply because it was only in 1989 that separation of the Associated Presbyterian Churches from the Free Presbyterian took place. The case for separation in 1893, if proved, will vindicate the one equally with the other at this point). No amount of flag waving and nostalgic speeches on the sacrifices both churches suffered in separating can be any substitute for a determined attempt to unfold the truth.

In the first place, I wish to establish the nature of a protest and the times when its use in church courts is appropriate. Secondly, I hope to verify the right for Mr Macfarlane and the other Constitutional ministers to remain in the Free Church without complicity in the Declaratory Act in 1892, even though the Act was passed under the Barrier Act in that year, and hence became a binding law and constitution, simply because they were under protest. I wish, then, to go on to show how a division took place between Mr Macfarlane and the other Constitutional ministers over the year 1892-93, so that his stance was not, indeed, identical with theirs by the Assembly of 1893, and to suggest that this is what caused Mr Macfarlane's separation in 1893, while the other Constitutional ministers remained where they were. I wish to show that the values emphasised by the Associated Presbyterian Churches were the values according to which Mr Macfarlane acted in his separation from the (1843) Free Church in 1893. That leads, finally, back to the point at which I start; the ownership of the manse in Kinlochbervie.

In his book, "No Great Mischief If You Fall", (1992) John Macleod the journalist says of me, rather charmingly, that in 1978 "he foolishly chose to immerse himself in the Charybdis of the Protest controversy. It is a feature of this recurring disease that victims come to consider the canon-law issue the most important facing Christendom; and each is certain that he understands it perfectly as none other before."

Mr MacLeod is dealing in the immediate context, (p. 114), with the 1978 case in which I took up a certain stance in relation to protest. He is, perhaps, influenced by the motion with which that case concluded - a motion which called on me to apply myself to "vital and ordinary duties" and not concern myself with matters on the level of "foolish questions and genealogies". The context in which these words are quoted in Mr MacLeod's book is the run-up to the case involving the Lord Chancellor, and since he was the originator of that motion, John MacLeod may feel he has sufficient authority to give no further serious consideration to my views, (which were not reported in the account in the "Synod Proceedings"). Without touching on all the ramifications, it is Mr MacLeod's own Free Church who are among the first on the scene claiming an understanding of protest such that Mr Macfarlane would be guilty of schism, together with all who followed him, if that understanding were correct. Prof. Cameron claims that the stance of the ministers who came out in 1900 was identical with that of Mr Macfarlane in 1893. The result was that those separating in 1893 did so schismatically, since they did not acknowledge the full value of the protest they were under to protect them from the force of the Declaratory Act. Those making up the (1900) Free Church did, and hence did not fall into the same error.

Every minister is under vows to oppose schism "notwithstanding of whatsoever persecution or trouble arise." Being under such a charge, I should be able to understand the Free Church position and be able to justify my own. I am arrogating to myself no more ambitious aim. Since freedom from the charge of schism depends solidly on an understanding of the import of protest, I am merely performing my duty.

PART I; LESSONS OF HISTORY

CHAPTER 3

SCRIPTURAL FOUNDATIONS

My aim in this chapter is to show the relation between the open door which the believer has to Christ and the rights of private judgement and liberty of conscience which lie at the foundation of the right of protest.

A protest arises from a contest of wills. On one side there is the will of God mediated through a person who, under God's teaching, exercises his right of private judgement to resolve a particular issue. On the other side, there is the will of an authority not so instructed which resists God's will. First, let us consider the mediation of God's will.

Christ says to Nathanael, (John 1;51), "Hereafter ye shall see heaven open, and the angels of God ascending and descending upon the Son of man." The reference is, clearly, to the experience of Jacob when he saw the vision in the desert.

"And he dreamed and behold a ladder set up upon the earth, and the top of it reached to heaven: and behold the angels of God ascending and descending on it. ...."

And Jacob awaked out of his sleep, and he said,
Surely the Lord is in this place; and I knew it not.....
This is none other but the house of God, and this is
the gate of heaven."

Christ is Immanuel, God with us, and like the ladder, links earth
and heaven. His voice is the voice of God bringing direct
communication from heaven. As that voice comes to Jacob by the
avenue of unmerited favour from God, so Christ brings the
message of God's favour to us. The ladder is not drawn up to
heaven again. Christ remains the ladder - the mediator - between
God and sinful man. As the angels ascend and descend on the
ladder, so on the basis of His unique relationship to both God and
man, our prayers ascend, and from God to us answers return.

It is particularly after Pentecost that the full implications of being
in direct communication with heaven are grasped by the
disciples. When opposed by the authorities for preaching the
gospel, in complete simplicity of faith they pray, "Stretch forth
thy hand and let signs and wonders be done through thy holy
child Jesus." The continuance of the open door is proved when
"the place was shaken where they were assembled together; and
they were all filled with the Holy Ghost, and they spake the word
of God with boldness."

This is an illustration of the right of private judgement in
exercise. The authorities say "Do not preach." The Scriptures
say in the second Psalm that God laughs. They do not depend on
the fallible judgement of men when they see clearly from the
Word of God where their duty lies. God's command overrides the
most authoritative voice of men. As the disciples have the right
of private judgement, so they have liberty of conscience to oppose
whatever would resist the call to obedience.

The above illustration pits the Church as a whole against the
unbelieving world. Liberty of conscience is operative also within

the Church when brother faces brother. Peter is called from heaven to go to Cornelius, a Gentile. To Peter, the Gentiles were still "common and unclean". To him alone came the message to go to the house of Cornelius, a Gentile. Should Peter go the rounds of the brethren like some modern-day politician, marking up the brethren for or against the mission and delay until at least a majority were persuaded of its lawfulness?

The words of Peter in an earlier instance, ("We ought to obey God rather than man"), apply here also. When he obeys Christ he exercises the right of private judgement. Peter "consults not with flesh and blood". He goes, and when later arraigned before his brethren, these brethren have to learn through Peter's own experience the will of God. They judge, and while judging, they themselves are judged and convicted. "What was I," says Peter, "that I could withstand God." "When they heard these things they held their peace and glorified God."

Christ commanded his disciples without apology or excuse while on earth. He excuses his disciples from obeying "commandments of men" by the mere authority of his word alone, since that word is final. ("In this place is one greater than the temple"). After His ascension he remains in communication with His disciples by His Spirit. Thus his sheep hear his voice and they know and follow him. A stranger will they not follow, and when coercion is brought to bear on them in issues that are essential to the faith, they must not yield.

Hence, the Church is related to Christ in two ways. Christ has set up courts within His Church and calls on members of the Church to obey those who have the rule over them. Presumably, it was before such a court Peter was called in Acts 11. Christ is also related to His Church directly by His Spirit. When thought of in the first relation of governing to governed, the Church leaders are said to make up the Ministerial Church, ministering Christ's will to His people, "the kirk hearing the voice of Christ, the only spiritual King, and being ruled by His laws." (2nd Book of Discipline, 1.7). When thought of as making up the Mystical Church, there are no intermediate courts between the individual and Christ. Christ may communicate with His Ministerial Church in an understanding of His will which embraces the whole court. In other cases the revelation may come through one individual, as it came through Peter. In an instance of this nature, the Church will show their own mystical union with Christ by acknowledging the voice of Christ through the individual. Their ministerial duty will then be discharged by acknowledging the rightness of the individual's claim. This took place in Acts 11, and again in the council of Jerusalem when James says of the insight given to Peter, "Simeon hath declared how God at the first did visit the Gentiles, to take out of them a people for his name. And to this agree the words of the prophets; as it is written, After this I will return and build again the tabernacle of David, which is fallen down, and I will build again the ruins of it and I will set it up etc.."

Essentially the same operation takes place when a minister is before his presbytery under call to another parish. In the judgement of the whole presbytery, the minister, it may be thought, should stay where he is. Nevertheless, he may so present his personal call from Christ as to persuade the presbytery that this is the will of God which they should endorse. Their ministerial duty then becomes the acknowledgement of the voice of Christ channeled, not through the court as a whole, whether as unanimous, or as a majority, but through the one individual whom they see as having received the will of God to transmit to them.

There is a third possibility. Supposing a person comes to a court persuaded that he has the will of God, and fails to persuade the court that this is so. For the court to expel such a man is a serious matter. Even a Jewish Court listens seriously to Gamaliel when he tells them that, though totally opposed to the preaching of Christ, they may be opposing God in going to extreme measures against the apostles.   Take the instance of Paul opposing, it would seem, the whole church in Antioch when they withdrew from eating with the Gentiles. (Gal. 2;11ff.). Paul was convinced that they did not walk "uprightly according to the truth of the gospel".   Supposing that instead of accepting Paul's view, they had set it out as a rule that no Jew could eat with the Gentiles. Where Paul is certain that they are going against "the truth of the gospel", he cannot fall in with their view. He is duty bound to his conscience still to assert his right to eat with Gentiles and, come what may, must still assert this claim.

It is not for him, in circumstances like these, to take into his calculations what view the court will take of such conduct. His duty is done when he has presented his protest. This, however, is not the end of the matter so far as the court itself is concerned. The court may be uncertain, as the Sanhedrin was uncertain, whether this is Christ's will or not.   To expel the protester may be tantamount to expeling one who carries God's voice to them. Instances like this are not unwanting in Scripture.   "Your brethren that hated you, that cast you out for my name's sake, said, Let the Lord be glorified: but he shall appear to your joy, and they shall be ashamed." In the light of this, a protester like Paul might be allowed to remain in the Church, exercising his liberty not to desist from eating with the Gentiles.

To a casual observer, it might seem that such a Church is hopelessly divided.   To a person who takes into account the mystical relation of the Church with Christ, it will be seen that while divided on earth, both sides are still united mystically in Christ.   Where both sides acknowledge Christ's headship, and are united in agreeing to follow the will of Christ when more fully revealed to either party, the disunity is apparent rather than real.

PART 1; LESSONS OF HISTORY

CHAPTER 4

LUTHER'S LEGACY

My next task after the examination of Scripture is to establish
that the issues that surround "Protest" are issues that can be
traced back to the Reformation. Without developing any
argument at this stage, I will drop in the description of protest as
over against dissent set out by Rev. John MacLeod, (afterwards
Principal MacLeod of Free Church College), in vol. 6 of the F.P.
Magazine, (p. 158). He is speaking of the 1892 Declaratory Act.

> "When new legislation like this comes to be made, it
> often happens that all the office-bearers are not of the
> same mind. Those who oppose it may enter either a
> dissent or a protest - the difference being that when
> they are able to co-operate with the section which put
> through the new statute, even though they oppose it,
> they will enter a dissent, to make it clear that it was
> against their mind that the matter was done; but if
> they cannot co-operate with the new legislation, it is a
> protest they raise, or, in other words, a protective
> witness to say that they cannot be obedient to the
> courts in the matter in hand."

At the Reformation there enters the doctrine of "the priesthood of all believers", which is virtually the doctrine of the open door from God and to God. This was a doctrine developed by Luther in his movement away from the despotic rule of the Medieval Church.

The development of the doctrine may be divided into five stages.

1. **The Supremacy of the Scriptures**. Luther emphasised the Scriptures as the sole source of living truth. In this he did not differ from many others such as the humanists like Erasmus, Reuchlin and Colet who called the Church to reformation, as in Erasmus' book, "In Praise of Folly" on the basis of the discrepancy between the teaching of Scripture and the practice of the Church.

The first serious combatant Luther met with on the side of the official Church was Prierias, master of the sacred palace at Rome. Here are their respective views on Scripture:

Prieras' principles:

> "Whoever relies not on the teaching of the Roman Church and of the Roman pontiff as the infallible rule of faith, from which the Holy Scriptures themselves derive their strength and their authority, is a heretic."

Luther' principles:

> "The first is this expression of St. Paul: 'Though we or an angel from heaven, preach any other gospel unto you than that which we have preached unto you, let him be accursed.'

> "The second is this passage from St Augustine to St. Jerome: *'I have learned to render to the canonical books alone the honour of believing most firmly that*

*none of them has erred; as for the others, I do not
believe in what they teach, simply because it is they
who teach them."* (D'Aubigne, "The Life and Times
of Martin Luther" pp. 144,146).

2. The Will Liberated from Bondage. The point on which
Luther diverged from the humanists was on Christian liberty.
This was evident in his early book, "On the Freedom of the
Christian Man", and in particular in his "Bondage of the Will"
written in opposition to the stance taken by Erasmus.   The
doctrinal position of Luther was, doubtless, owing much to his
own personal experience. He had found all the ritualistic means
ordained by the Church totally unavailing to relieve his burdened
conscience. Luther found genuine relief only when he studied the
Scriptures and found in the experience of such as Paul the same
desperation. "The law is holy, just and good. I am carnal, sold
under sin." As Paul was delivered only by Christ as revealed by
the Spirit, so Luther.

3. Private Judgement. The above experience led Luther to a
new view of the relation of the believer to the Scriptures.
Doubtless, common sense, allied to acute scholarship, could
enable the humanists to give incisive criticism of many practices
in the Church of Rome. Nevertheless, the person who has been
brought to belief through the guidance of God's Spirit has a
unique key to these Scriptures. This insight became the
Reformation distinctive of the right of private interpretation of the
Scriptures.   Inevitably this brought Luther to clash with the
accepted view of the Church which regarded the Church, itself,
as the body which alone could interpret the Scriptures and hand
down that interpretation for implicit acceptance by the faithful.
"If mother Church errs in her censures, said he, we should still
honour her as Christ honoured Caiaphas, Annas, and
Pilate....Only God can sever spiritual communion. No creature
can separate us from the love of Christ." Bainton, "Here I stand"

p. 68. Christ, speaking through the Scriptures, gives liberty to the sinner. The same Scriptures under the teaching of Christ are the medium by which God communicates with the believer. "Ye have an unction from the Holy One, and ye know all things" said John to his readers. That knowledge was not given separate from the Scriptures. It was the basis for the doctrine of "private judgement".

The gift of the Spirit is necessary to stress at this point, since otherwise every man could claim right to his own private judgement. "All thy children shall be taught of the Lord," says Isaiah, "and great shall be the peace of they children," (Isa. 54;13). It is those who have benefited from that teaching who are the "spiritual" of 1 Corinthians. Such a man "judgeth all things, yet he, himself, is judged of no man." Such have "the mind of Christ." (1 Cor. 2;15,16).

As priests in the Old Testament were consecrated with anointing oil, so New Testament believers are anointed with the Spirit.

4. **Liberty to Serve**. The other side of the priesthood of all believers is that as priests offered up sacrifices to God in Old Testament times, so the believer of New Testament times offers up spiritual sacrifices "holy and acceptable by Christ Jesus." All service to God out of "child-like love and a willing heart" is a spiritual, acceptable sacrifice.

5. **Liberty from Oppressive Rule.** Christ being the head of each individual believer, Luther was bold to oppose the might of the organised Church where he considered that that Church stood between him and the service of God. Celibacy of the clergy, the mass, monasticism, worship of Mary, the uniqueness of the papacy must go. There is no treasury of saints which beleaguered Christians may draw upon, and the relics which claim to act as a channel of such merits are a fiction, also.

It was in the spirit of these five points that Luther at the Diet of Worms refused to comply with the call of the court to recant. When asked if he repudiated his books and the errors which they contained, Luther replied, "Since then Your Majesty and your lordships desire a simple reply, I will answer without horns and without teeth. Unless I am convicted by Scripture and plain reason - I do not accept the authority of popes and councils, for they have contradicted each other - my conscience is captive to the word of God. I cannot and I will not recant anything, for to go against conscience is neither right nor safe. God help me. Amen." (Bainton, p. 144).

That is of the essence of ecclesiastical protest. *It is a conscientious refusal not only to agree with views contrary to Scripture, (dissent), but to submit to unscriptural commands in practice because one's conscience is held in thrall to the word of God. Whether that leads to separation or not does not depend on the protester. It depends on whether the tribunal addressed will allow such liberty without forcing the protester into separation.*

The Constitutional minority in 1892 were in the same situation as Luther at Worms. The Declaratory Act undermined Scripture. Conscientiously, they could not submit to it. Hence, they said in their protest that the Act would not be binding upon them. When inscribed on the books of the Assembly, the protest became what Rev. John MacLeod would call a "protective witness", safeguarding them from the action of the Act. A dissent could not have served the same purpose.

The realised embodiment of these doctrines may take different forms in different branches of Protestantism. Luther veered towards giving magistrates the rule over the Church since "magistrates were fellow Christians sharing in the priesthood of all believers." (Bainton p.118). The relevant embodiment of these doctrines for the Presbyterian is that in the Westminster Confession of Faith which became the doctrinal standard for the Church of Scotland in 1647.

PART 1: LESSONS OF HISTORY

CHAPTER 5

CONFESSIONAL GUIDELINES

At the Diet of Worms, Luther was a single voice asserting his right of private judgement against the autocratic claims of the Church of Rome. In a sense, this was the easier part. At this point he was exercising the luxury of criticism without having the responsibility of rule. When he returned to Wittenberg to begin his own reformation, the question was how to place that right of private judgement in the context of the undoubted authority of the Church to exercise rule.

That question, so far as the Lutheran Church is concerned, need not detain us. The story as it concerns us is the question of how the Reformed Church in Scotland met these difficulties.

In 1647, the Church adopted the Westminster Confession of Faith. I wish now to consider how the Confession handles each of the five distinctives which have already been traced in the development of Luther's stance as he progressively moved to an independent position, and how the Confession fits these into the operation of Church life.

1. **The supremacy of Scripture.**

"Under the name of Holy Scripture, or the Word of God written, are now contained all the books of the Old and New Testaments, which are these:-

Genesis, Exodus, etc. ....Revelation.

All which are given by inspiration of God, to be the rule of faith and life." (1.II).

"The authority of the holy scripture, for which it ought to be believed and obeyed, dependeth not upon the testimony of any man or church, but wholly upon God, who is truth itself,) and the author thereof; and therefore it is to be received, because it is the word of God." (1.V).

"The infallible rule of interpretation of scripture is the scripture itself; and therefore when there is a question about the true and full sense of any scripture, (which is not manifold but one), it must be searched and known by other places that speak more clearly.
"The supreme judge by which all controversies of religion are to be determined, and all decrees of councils, opinions of ancient writers, doctrines of men and private spirits, are to be examined, and in whose sentence we are to rest, can be no other than the Holy Spirit speaking in scripture." (1.IX,X).

These views on the supremacy of holy scripture, on the rejection of the need of views handed down on the authority of the Church for implicit acceptance, on the right to give no credence to councils no matter how venerated or how ancient if they contradict scripture, are fully in accordance with the views of Luther outlined in the previous chapter.

2. Christian liberty.

"The liberty which Christ hath purchased for believers under the gospel, consists in their freedom from the guilt of sin, the condemning wrath of God, the curse of the moral law; and their being delivered from this present evil world, bondage to Satan, and dominion of sin, from the evil of afflictions, the sting of death, the victory of the grave and everlasting damnation."

That the above words speak of the first side of the priesthood of believers is evident if one thinks of the words of Christ, "The Spirit of the Lord God is upon me; because the Lord hath anointed me to preach good tidings unto the meek, he hath sent me to bind up the broken-hearted, to proclaim liberty to the captives, and the opening of the prison to them that are bound." As Christ is anointed himself, so he anoints sinners to receive liberty through Him.

3. Private Judgement.

The Confession acknowledges that there are many internal arguments whereby the scripture "doth abundantly evidence itself to be the word of God." (1.V). "Nevertheless, we acknowledge the inward illumination of the Spirit of God to be necessary for the saving understanding of such things as are revealed in the word." (1.VI). This true judgement of the truth of Scripture is bound up with the Christian Liberty mentioned above. "The god of this world blinds the minds of those who believe not", says Paul. Conversely, it is as liberated from this god of the world that we are brought to saving understanding. The same could be said about liberation from the world, ("the lust of the flesh, the lust of the eye, and the pride of life"). It is when these beams are taken from our eyes by the Spirit of God that we will see clearly. "Our full persuasion and assurance of the infallible truth, and divine authority thereof, is from the inward work of the Holy Spirit, bearing witness by and with the word in our hearts." (I.V). Hence, the gift of private judgement is not confined to that part of scripture by which at first we came to faith, but extends itself, more or less, to the scriptures as a whole. In the case of the Ethiopian eunuch, it was through one verse of Isaiah 53 that his eyes were opened. Nevertheless, one can imagine that the enlightenment gained through this one verse would act as a key to unlock the whole message of Isaiah and the other scriptures, also.

4. New Obedience.

The new obedience is the other side of Christian liberty. As the anointing of the Spirit gives liberty *from* so it gives liberty *to*. "The liberty which Christ hath purchased for believers under the gospel consists in" (here follows the part quoted above) "as also in their free access to God, and their yielding obedience unto him, not out of slavish fear, but a child-like love and willing mind." Now the priest, having received the anointing of the Spirit, offers up "spiritual sacrifices acceptable to God by Jesus Christ." "Whatsoever is not of faith is sin." Conversely, what is of faith, even a cup of cold water in the name of a disciple, is a spiritual sacrifice.

5. Liberty of Conscience from implicit faith in, and and absolute and blind obedience to, pronouncements contrary to or beside the Word of God, i.e. from oppressive rule.

If "the whole counsel of God, concerning all things necessary for his own glory, man's salvation, faith and life, is either expressly set down in scripture, or by good and necessary consequence may be deduced from scripture", (1.VI), then the believer under the enlightenment of the Spirit, has all that is required to enable him to judge his duty, and to reject what might lead him astray. It is no wonder, then, that the section following Christian liberty deals with Liberty of conscience. "God alone is lord of the conscience, and hath left it free from the doctrines and commandments of men which are in anything contrary to his word, or beside it in matters of faith or worship. So that to believe such doctrines or to obey such commandments out of conscience is to betray true liberty of conscience: and the requiring of an implicit faith, and an absolute and blind obedience, is to destroy liberty of conscience, and reason also."

We have now reached the stance of Luther at the Diet of Worms. On the basis of a true spiritual understanding of the scriptures, he rejects the infallible authority of the Pope and the laws regarded by him as either contravening Scripture, or else left by Scripture as an open question. This still leaves the issue of official Church authority unanswered. As Luther had to face the question of the exercise of authority by church courts, so the Confession has yet to pronounce on how authority can be maintained in the Scottish Reformed Church if every man is to be his own judge.

In section IV of chapter XX, there is a strong rebuttal of the right of licence when it masquerades under the guise of liberty of conscience. Not only may the church authorities unmask such imposture, but they are bound to proceed against it by the censures of the church, and by the power of the civil magistrate. It may seem we are almost back to the autocracy of the Church of Rome once again. The courts may use their liberty of conscience on their side, their right of private judgement, their ability to assess the truth of Scripture, their stance under Christ the head of the Church, to suppress error. The great difficulty is that that is what many in the Roman Catholic Church thought they were doing when they condemned Luther. Who is to guarantee that, when Paul admits that Christians, themselves, may become "carnal, and walk as men", a court of such men may not condemn a person who is truly spiritual? That the Confession is not unconscious of the difficulty is evident when it prefaces the above passage by the words, "And because the powers which God hath ordained, and the liberty which Christ hath purchased, are not intended by God to destroy, but mutually to uphold one another, etc.". There is to be a balance. It is clear that this passage envisages times of conflict, or there would be no danger of one destroying the other. On the one side, the powers which rule are not to be crippled by a cacophony of assertions of the right to exercise Christian liberty by each individual member of a court. Equally, these courts are not to be so intent on uniformity that all freedom of individual expression is suppressed.

The practical way in which this is to be done is outlined in the XXXIst chapter.

"It belongeth to synods and councils ministerially to determine controversies of faith, and cases of conscience; to set down rules and directions for the better ordering of the worship of God, and government of his church; to receive complaints in cases of mal-administration, and authoritatively to determine the same; which decrees and determinations, *if consonant to the word of God*, are to be received with reverence and submission, not only for their agreement with the word, but also for the power whereby they are made, as being an ordinance of God, appointed thereunto in his word."

The individual believer is not to be put off with the assertion, "You believe the Bible is the word of God. If you search that word with submission and humility, you will see that there are commands such as these, 'Submit yourselves to every ordinance of man for the Lord's sake', (1 Peter 2;13), or 'Obey them that rule over you, and submit yourselves, for they watch for your souls etc.' (Heb. 13;17). These commands show the need for absolute submission to those who have been entrusted with you spiritual care." The private judgement of the believer is to be engaged at an earlier stage. As he has the right to examine the substance of decrees and determinations of earlier synods and councils, and measure their content by the yardstick of Scripture, so current decrees must be examined by the same rule. In this way, the powers that rule may not obliterate private judgement. Only if decrees and determinations are in accord with the Scriptures is he to give them reverence and submission. Not surprisingly, then, in view of the fact that "All councils since the apostles' times, whether general or particular, may err, and many have erred; therefore they are not to be made the rule of faith or practice, but to be used as an help in both."

There is a great difference between being used as an help, and being absolutely regulative.

The fore-going statement, of course, has relevance to the position of the minority in 1892 when the Declaratory Act was passed. It was quite permissible for them to examine the Act and judge whether or not it was according to Scripture. If it was not, it must not be made a rule of faith or practice. The Free Church authorities, on their side, must not demand implicit faith or absolute and blind obedience. They must make provision for the exercise of Scriptural liberty of conscience. It will be seen that both took place. The Church authorities in the drafting of the Act made implied provision for the exercise of liberty of conscience, and the minority took advantage of this in indicating that the Act would not be binding on them. The Supreme Court then confirmed the right of the protesting minority by accepting their protest and inscribing it on the books of the Assembly.

PART 1; LESSONS OF HISTORY

CHAPTER 6

NO RIGID UNIFORMITY

The Confession of Faith was approved in 1647. The Questions and Formula by which office-bearers were bound to the Confession of Faith as the confession of their faith dates from 1711, after the attempt to impose episcopacy on the Scottish Church had been defeated. Taylor Innes suggests that the stringency with which the Confession of Faith was bound on the subscribers stemmed from " a vague but strong dread of heresy." (pp. 86,87).

Whatever the case, the great difficulty in supporting such views on private judgement as have been outlined in previous chapters, is that they might seem to run directly in the teeth of the vows which probationers take when they become ministers over congregations.

"Do you promise to submit yourself willingly and humbly, in the spirit of meekness, unto the admonitions of the brethren of this Presbytery, and to be subject to them, and all other Presbyteries and superior judicatories of this Church, where God in his providence shall cast your lot; and that according to your power, you shall maintain the unity and peace of this Church against error and schism, notwithstanding of whatsoever trouble or persecution may arise, and that you shall follow no divisive courses from the doctrine, worship, discipline and government of this Church?" (Montcrieff, The Practice of the Free Church of Scotland, 4th edition p. 157.)

At one stroke, it may seem that all that has been said about the active power of Christ on earth, his empowering of individual office-bearers to examine and reject laws contrary to their liberty of private judgement is taken away. Rigid conformity to the will of the majority is the absolute duty of each office-bearer.

To say this is to take a very superficial view of these vows, and of the point at which obedience is required. The Confession of Faith says, "The powers which God hath ordained, and the liberty which Christ hath purchased, are not intended to destroy, but mutually to uphold one another." Only at the point where it is evident that full value has been given to a conscientious disagreement is it required that the minister who comes under vows must submit. It is the Confession, itself, that says that decrees and determinations are not to be made a rule but a help in matters of faith and conduct. Therefore any minister has a right to claim these privileges. The ministers who are his co-presbyters and who may become his judges in any dispute are bound by the same Confession. Therefore they, on their side, are bound to allow him his rights.

The practical outworking of this in the life of the Church was seen in the fact that decrees passed at one Assembly were not automatically binding. They had the power of directing life and conduct without enforcing. In 1639 an Act was passed which was aimed at ensuring the passage of binding laws when these were required. The careful way in which this Act, the first Barrier Act, was worded, however, shows the concern the

Reformers of the second Reformation had that while necessity may have been laid on them to pass certain laws of a binding nature, they were concerned at the same time that the rights of conscience of any minority would not be overridden.

> "That no innovation which may disturb the peace of the Church and make division be suddenly proposed and enacted, but so as the motion be first communicated to the several synods, presbyteries, and kirk-sessions, that the matter may be approved by all at home, and commissioners may come well prepared, unanimously to conclude a solid deliberation upon these points in the General Assembly."

The second Barrier Act, 1697, at the end of the same century was less kind to tender consciences. The Act made quite explicit that it referred to "binding laws and constitutions." There was no mention of unanimous consent. It required only a majority in favour of an overture in order for that overture to become binding, having passed through the presbyteries the previous year for their consideration. The fact remained, however, that resolutions passed at only one Assembly were not binding.

It must be clear, however, that even such an Act as the Barrier Act could introduce binding constitutions only in relation to such laws as had sanction from the Scriptures. It still remained the constitutional right of the believer not to make decrees which were not consonant with the word of God, "the rule of faith or practice," whether these had passed through the Barrier Act or not. If one admitted the right of courts to make ordinances binding which called for absolute and blind obedience merely on the will of the Court itself, one would be back with the despotic rule from which the Reformers thought they had escaped.

In the light of these truths, the rights of the individual office-bearer are secured. Indeed, if he found the Church did not uphold Christian liberty, an office-bearer who disagreed with his Church in this regard would have a perfect right to oppose the Church, deriving this right from the ordination vows themselves. He is to oppose error, "notwithstanding of whatsoever trouble or persecution may arise". When courts seek to impose implicit faith, or seek to bind by an absolute and blind obedience, they are in error and must be opposed.

The Dangers of Schism.

If there is a failure to reach conformity, would it not be an act of charity in the person who is failing to conform to leave the church with the minimum of fuss? The continuance of his presence will only cause an abiding irritation, both to himself and to those he disagrees with. In application to the situation in 1892, should not the Constitutional Party have withdrawn quietly from the Free Church without fuss having made clear their irreconcilable opposition to the Declaratory Act.

Where the Church in question is maintaining a consistent witness to the fundamental doctrines contained in the Confession of Faith, and the office-bearer cannot agree with these fundamental doctrines, such as the doctrine of the Trinity, or the deity of Christ, will be evident that separation must follow. Apart from such a clear case, there are a variety of reasons why it may be the duty of the person to remain where he is.

(i) He may be required to remain as God's faithful witness in a deteriorating situation. That was the kind of situation Jeremiah found himself in. He sat alone because of God's hand wishing for wings to fly away like a dove, and charging God with making his pain perpetual. God told him simply to return and to act as his mouth, taking the precious from the vile.

The ordination vows themselves give a reason why such witnesses should remain. Not only do ordination vows call on office-bearers to resist error "whatsoever trouble or persecution may arise." They are to oppose schism likewise, and to the same degree. The obvious fruit of this is that they must seek to prevent unnecessary separation. The office-bearers who make up the court which sits in judgement on any individual must likewise oppose unnecessary separation. In 1892, the General Assembly made allowance for the exercise of liberty of conscience. It would have been schismatic to depart in such circumstances.

ii.   There is another reason for remaining. Where absolute and blind obedience or implicit faith are required, there men are made the "lords of faith and conscience." In such a case, Christ cannot have the pre-eminence. It is remarkable how Paul refused to circumcise Titus for this very reason. False brethren came in privily to spy out "our liberty which we have in Christ Jesus, that they might bring us into bondage." The matter might seem a relatively trivial issue, especially since Paul had previously circumcised Timothy lest he give offence to the Jews.   He gives the reason as follows, "To whom we gave place by subjection, no, not for an hour; that the truth of the gospel might continue with you." If one who has a justified conviction gives way to those who would lord it over him, the gospel, itself, will depart if he either submits or departs from his post of duty, and lets the "lords of faith and conscience" have their way. As soon as courts begin to love to have the pre-eminence, and reveal this in abandoning their role to exercise government "in consonance ... with the liberties of his (Christ's) people" ("Claim, Declaration and Protest") , so soon may they freely be disobeyed, just as surely as the apostle John invited Gaius to disobey the courts over which Diotrephes loved to have the pre-eminence by receiving John and other brethren as visitors. (3 John 9,10 and 5,14). If and when men begin to have dominion over our faith, Christ is expelled.

iii. A third reason is, the need for continuing reformation. The Reformation began with Luther adopting a stance of "Here I stand, I can do no other. So help me God." Unlike the "Always the same" motto of the Church of Rome, the Protestant church has adopted the motto, "Always Requiring to be Reformed". This continuing reformation can only be carried into effect when men adopt the stance of Luther in opposition to burdens placed on their consciences by the courts of the churches under which they operate. Luther did not immediately leave without seeking to reform from within. So neither should they.

These considerations increase the obligation to preserve a healthy lack of uniformity in practice within the Church rather than to drive those who differ on relatively minor points outside the pale.

Where does this leave the courts of the Church when dealing with a particular case? The centre from which the court always acts is Scripture. The limits of what is right according to the light they have at the time in the view of the court, will fall within one circle. The limits of what is admissible because it is an exercise of genuine liberty of conscience will form a larger, concentric circle. The first circle represents the court's judgement of Scripture according to the light they have at that time. The second circle represents the possibilities they see that there may be another admissible interpretation. There are matters that a court may, in their opinion, consider wrong because they lie outside the first circle, but which may be allowed because within the larger. The fact the Assembly in 1892 accepted the protest offered by the Constitutional minority, and inscribed it in the Assembly's books directly after the terms of the Declaratory Act, itself, seems to indicate they were aware of the necessity of taking the second step of considering whether the action might be a legitimate exercise of liberty of conscience, even though it ran directly counter to the Declaratory Act which had just been passed.

PART 2: DISRUPTION WORTHIES

CHAPTER 1

THEIR PRINCIPLES:
THE MODERATE/ EVANGELICAL STRUGGLE

In 1687, Isaac Newton with his "Principia Mathematica" applied a few basic principles to the physical working of the universe and revealed that behind apparent incomprehensible complexity lay a relatively simple pattern within the reach of every thinking man. It is not surprising that theology felt the impact. Eight years later, a book from the pen of John Locke, "The Reasonableness of Christianity", claimed that the fundamental truths of Christianity were equally few and simple and within the reach of all. The order of the universe witnessed to God's existence, wisdom and goodness. It was to be expected that such a God would give a special revelation. This revelation was found in the Bible, and it confirmed the truths already deduced from nature.

It is likewise not surprising that such teaching soon found itself in conflict with the Bible. Deriving its inspiration from the reasonableness of nature, it took unkindly to any teaching within Scripture which seemed unreasonable.

Consider Thomas Chalmers who began his ministry under the influence of such views. In a sermon on "Human Duty" based on Micah 6;8, he makes Nature, reason and virtue the yardstick of truth.

> "We recognise the faith of Christianity as that which
> is derived from the force of reason, and the energy of

virtuous sentiment." "Let us therefore pray the Father of Spirits that He would dispel those clouds of ignorance and error which overwhelm the nations; that He would enable them to see the religion of Jesus in its native purity. ... They will learn to admire and imitate the rational and elevated piety, the ardent charity, the pure and exalted virtue of Jesus and his apostles."

At this point, Chalmers rejects vicarious atonement;

"Perhaps the God of Nature meant to illustrate the purity of His perfection to the children of men" (in the death of Christ). ...."The tenets of those whose gloomy and unenlarged minds are apt to imagine that the Author of Nature required the death of Jesus merely for the reparation of violated justice, are rejected by all free and rational enquirers." (Biog. vol. 1, p. 147)

More to the point for the purpose of our study, Chalmers had no place for the open door as I have described it. Reason and virtue are sufficient to guide man. He fulminates against those who have "attached the highest degree of importance to those doctrines which transcend the limits of our faculties."

"The faith of Christianity is praiseworthy and meritorious only because it is derived from the influence of virtuous sentiments on the mind. Hence the labours of those are grossly misapplied who inculcate the belief of certain religious truths as the method of obtaining the favour of heaven."

Where men have already an open door to God by the exercise of native reason and virtue, Christian liberty from the curse of the law, or the bondage of Satan is superfluous.

Chalmers at this stage of his life was a "Moderate." In the Highlands such were called "ministearean maide" - "wooden ministers", since they had no ringing gospel to proclaim, no "beauty for ashes to offer, or opening of the prison for those who were bound." William Hogarth, the English caricaturist, at about the same period depicts a bewigged clergyman of this school reading through a sermon with the ironical title, "Come unto me and I will give you rest." Throughout the church building, in various ungainly poses, his congregation are sound asleep. At the opposite extreme was the Evangelical, men of the calibre of Whitfield and Wesley in Scotland or the Erskines and Boston in Scotland. Such ministers did not begin with the order of nature and then move on to the Scriptures to supplement their views. They began with Scripture and sought to interpret the Scripture message in its own light.

Thomas Chalmers is an interesting case, because a few years after preaching the above sermon he had an illness, and emerged an Evangelical.

> "I am now most thoroughly of opinion, and it is an opinion founded on experience, that on the system of - Do this and live, no peace, and even no true and worthy obedience, can ever be attained. It is, Believe in the Lord Jesus Christ and thou shalt be saved. When this belief enters the heart, joy and confidence enter along with it. We look to God in a new light - we see him as a reconciled Father; that love to Him which terror scares away re-enters the heart, and, with a new principle and a new power, we become new creatures in Christ Jesus our Lord." (Biog. p. 186).

Here is a re-duplication of Luther's experience of the open door. Chalmers had moved from an easy complacency to an experience of that "terror of the Lord", just as Luther did, which results from seeing his inadequacy to meet the demands of a holy God. He had experienced the entry of joy and confidence through the Spirit of Christ driving out that terror through the open door which faith in His grace reveals. He is now a new creature ready to offer up spiritual sacrifices acceptable by Christ Jesus.

It is not surprising that, with two mutually opposing views of the Christian experience, the two sides should have equally opposing views on a whole variety of topics.

They were opposed on the nature of the ministry. The Moderate minister was often cultured, but since the mind of God was read in nature, and since God in his view was a kind of absentee landlord, doctrines like the unique transforming power of Christ turning men from darkness to light were dubbed with the name of "enthusiasm." His commission was to instruct and inform. The Evangelical, by contrast, felt a calling, under the constraint of the redeeming love of Christ, to beseech men, "Be ye reconciled to God."

Their views of Christ, Himself, differed. Of those who "exclaim with exultation, Lo, the Spirit of Jesus is in us", the moderate Chalmers says, "Oh, my soul, come not thou into their secret." To those of the Evangelical persuasion, to whom the presence of Christ, "walking among the candlesticks," has become a living reality, this is of the essence of their faith.

The functions of the Scriptures have changed for the Evangelical. After quoting "If any man have not the Spirit of Christ, he is none of his," the now evangelical Chalmers says, "If the Bible will not convince, little can be done by a mere human interpreter; and nothing remains but to deplore the delusion which I cannot rectify - to pity and to pray for it." (Sermons, 1798-1847).

All these points mean there will be an entirely different approach to the question of the choice of ministers to a particular parish. The Evangelical, seeing the ministry charged with a unique embassage from God, will require that they be men who can say, "I believe, and therefore I have spoken." Mere culture and learning will not suffice. Having a high view of Scripture, they will believe that Scripture must be appealed to to find out how the choice of ministers be made. Believing that the ordinary believer lives in fellowship with Christ, he will judge that he has the means by virtue of that indwelling to judge the suitability of those set over him in spiritual things. Church courts exist not only to act under Christ for the good of the Church, but to ensure that those liberties given by Christ are safeguarded to the members of the Church.

> "The Lord Jesus .... has invested the ordinary members of His church with important spiritual privileges, and as called them to exercise, on their own responsibility, important spiritual functions. In particular, we are persuaded that their consent, either formally given, or inferred from the absence of dissent, ought to be regarded by the church officers as an indispensable condition in forming the pastoral relation." (Evangelical Engagement, 1840).

During the 18th century, the law of the land for the appointment of ministers was the Patronage Act of 1712. This meant that ministers were appointed by the patron, usually the landowner. However few signed the call, the right of the patron to present a candidate to a particular parish, and insist that his choice be received, (provided the candidate was otherwise qualified), was paramount.

Certain presbyters of the Evangelical Party would conscientiously refuse to take part in the induction of a presentee when the people clearly opposed the appointment. Such, by custom, were allowed to distance themselves from the whole proceedings. Sufficient ministers might not be present in a particular presbytery to induct the minister in question to his new charge. In such a case, the General Assembly had hitherto taken a lenient view. A "Riding Committee" was appointed made up of members of other presbyteries who were given power to carry through the induction.

Gradually the Moderate Party became more and more strident in demanding that ministers, whatever their conscientious scruples, be present to carry out inductions. The Evangelical Party drew up a defence of what they considered their rights.

The following is their manifesto. It originated as Reasons of Dissent, entered on the 15th of May, 1751, from the sentence of the General Assembly, censuring the Rev. members of the presbytery of Linlithgow, for not executing the sentences of former Assemblies, appointing them to ordain and admit Mr James Watson, minister of the parish of Torphichen.

"Whatever privileges the Church of Scotland has by law, these can never make her a merely voluntary, or merely legal society, so as to be governed only by rules of her own making, or only by civil laws, or only by both together; but she must still be reckoned a part of the church of Christ, of which he alone is Lord and King; and which has a government appointed by him, distinct from the civil magistracy; and all the members of it are to be subject to his laws alone, absolutely and without reserve. And therefore we think the censures of the church are never to be inflicted but upon open transgressors of the laws of Christ, himself, its only lawgiver; nor can we think that any man is to be constructed an open transgressor of the laws of Christ, merely for not obeying commands of any assembly of fallible men; when he declares it was a conscientious regard to the will of Christ, himself, that led him to this disobedience.

And therefore this decision of the Assembly seems to us a stretch of power derogatory to the rights of conscience, of which God alone is Lord; and to the sole authority of Christ in his church.

2. We have always .... conceived that Presbyterian government, as distinguished from all other forms of church government consisted in the parity of pastors and subordination of church judicatures; as it is described both in the form of our subscription and in the laws of our establishment; without implying that even the supreme judicature was vested with absolute authority or infallibility, or that an active obedience without reserve was to be given to its decisions; which we could never imagine to be a principle tenable by any Christian Protestant church. Accordingly, our subscription, and engagement to obedience and submission to the judicatures of the church, is with the express limitation of its being in the Lord; that is, in such cases only as we judge not to be disagreeable to the will of the Lord: of which every man has an unalienable right to judge for himself, as he will be answerable to the Lord: a right which he cannot give up to any man or society of men; BECAUSE IT IS NOT MERELY HIS PRIVILEGE BUT HIS INALIENABLE DUTY:

3. (Conclusion based on above premises).

Will Wishart, D.D. Principal of the College of Edinburgh, and other 22 ministers.

Here we are presented with the same emphases as in preceding chapters. Effective government must not rule out the rights of individual consciences. If we have government which calls for total, blanket obedience, what room is there for the exercise of private judgement and liberty of conscience? The right of liberty was asserted on two fronts. The Church had the right to oppose the law of the land. Within the Church, those who strove for the application of Scriptural principles to ordination and induction had the right of at least passive resistance to the application of the law of patronage.

The Moderates replied at great length. All the arguments are simply variants of the following:

> "By joining together in society, we enjoy many advantages which we could neither purchase nor secure in a disunited state. In consideraton of these, we consent that regulations for public order shall be established; not by the private fancy of every individual, but by the judgement of the majority, or of those with whom the society has consented to entrust the legislative power. Their judgement must necessarily be absolute and final, and their decisions received as the voice and injunction of the whole."

If it be asked which side of the debate the Free Presbyterian Church should favour, the following should suffice:

> "The Free Presbyterian Church maintains most emphatically that no authority in the hands of fallible men, such as the authority of the Synod, has any absolute rule over the consciences of believers."

Manual of Practice, p. 66.

The Evangelical Party became more influential in the councils of the Church of Scotland until it was able to pass into law in 1834 the Veto Act which resolved that no call would be valid which was opposed by the majority of the male heads of families in the parish. At the Disruption, this body separated to become the Free Church. From it, the F. P. Church claims direct connection.

PART 2; DISRUPTION WORTHIES

CHAPTER 2

THE DISRUPTION

A proof of the rights of private judgement and liberty of conscience may be drawn from the Claim, Declaration and Protest of 1842.

When the Evangelical party gained the upper hand in 1833, as it was mentioned they did in the previous chapter, they determined to put an end to the evils of lay patronage, and the intrusion of ministers into parishes by the aid of the secular authority. They passed a Veto Act, aiming to give back to the call of the people a significant place in the settlement of a minister. It provided that the majority of dissentient voices would be a veto on any presentation. Defeated in the Assembly of 1833, it passed in 1834 and became a standing law in 1835.

The whole Church of Scotland opposed patronage. What made the Evangelical Party differ from the Moderate, was that they considered that in matters of conscience obedience must be rendered at all costs to Christ. It will be seen that so long as the Moderate Party was dominant, obedience to the State was not the main issue. The Moderate Party believed in submission. The Moderate Party had the majority in the Assembly. Rulings made by use of this majority became the judgement of the Church as a whole. It was these rulings the State had to deal with. It was within the Church debate raged, when individuals could not submit to their ecclesiastical superiors. When the Evangelical Party won the ascendancy, the positions were reversed. The decisions of the Evangelical majority became the decisions of the Assembly, and it was with these decisions the State had to deal directly. It will also be seen that, taking the view as they did that individuals are bound to follow conscience, a confrontation was unavoidable with the State, unless a prior and workable arrangement were come to by which the Gordian knot of patronage were resolved. It was hoped that the Veto Act would provide such a solution.

In an Established Church, the Church operates in partnership with the State. Why, then, was this law passed without prior consultation with Parliament? The answer was that the Evangelical Party thought that they were acting within the law as it stood.

Over the years when patronage held full sway, the call had become an irrelevance. It did not matter how many or how few signed the call, the induction of the presentee of the patron went ahead, provided he were "qualified". A man was qualified if he were acceptable in life and doctrine. The Evangelicals extended the reach of the word, "qualified" to take in a qualification which had never altogether vanished out of sight, viz. the call of the people. This revival of the call was not thought to involve a challenge to the law, but rather a change of emphasis.

In 1839, the House of Lords declared the Veto Act illegal. The word "qualified", in their opinion, confined itself to the personal qualifications of the presentee, i.e. to his life, literature and manners. It was unlawful to extend it to the call of the people.

The Moderate Party had been in agreement with the Veto Act. When the State now showed itself frankly in opposition to the Veto Act, the difference in the outlook of the Moderate section of the Assembly and the Evangelical began to express itself once again, in accordance with the principles each respectively held. The Moderate called for absolute submission to the civil courts. The Evangelical claimed liberty of conscience under the headship of Christ to uphold the Veto Act in defiance of the civil courts.

In the General Assembly which followed that same month, Dr. Cook, the leader of the Moderate Party, moved that the Assembly should hold the Veto Law as abrogated, and proceed as if it never had passed. The Church, in Dr Cook's view, was virtually a creature of the State in issues in which the State had an interest. Dr Chalmers, the leader of the Evangelical Party, was most decidedly convinced of the independent sphere of the Church in ruling over her people. She was not under the direction of the State, and whatever laws the State might be pleased to pass, but under the direction of Christ.

> "It (the Church) may have subsisted for many ages as a Christian Church, with all its tenets and its usages, not as prescribed by human authority, but as founded whether on the word of God or on their own independent views of Christian expediency - meaning by this their own views of what is best for the good of imperishable souls. None of these things were given up to the State at the time when the Church entered into alliance with it."

In such an impasse between State and Church, why did separation not follow immediately? There are at least two answers. One is that it was an awesome responsibility to disrupt the National

Church. All the arguments against schism already laid down in Part 1, ch. 6 were against it. The other was that the very arguments stemming from liberty of conscience which made it imperative for the Evangelicals to oppose the Act of Patronage, legitimised a debate in which she could invoke the authority of that source, and enter into dialogue with the State on the basis of that authority. That is what the Church proceeded to do.

Between 1839 and 1842, the Church sought to have the law amended so that her principles were acknowledged. By 1842 it was evident that the attempts to have the law amended had failed, and there was no way that their principles could be given place within the law as it stood. An Anti-patronage Act was carried in the Assembly. Yet even at this late date, separation did not take place immediately. The Church made it clear in the Claim, Declaration and Protest drawn up and approved at the 1842 Assembly that there was a way forward. If the State would acknowledge her principle that it is Christ the Church must obey, "not out of slavish fear, but a child-like love and willing mind", and that in this situation she has a right of appeal to Christ - an appeal which the State should respect - then she would submissively surrender the temporalities. Thus the real point at issue for the Church is singled out. Will the State acknowledge the liberty of the Church under her heavenly King to judge privately what her duty is in the light of Scripture teaching, to resist submission to laws which would cause her to surrender her liberty, and to appeal to the living Christ, the Head of the Church, to resolve this issue?

> "And they declare that they cannot, in accordance with the word of God, the authorised and ratified standards of this Church, intrude ministers on reclaiming congregations, or carry on the government of Christ's Church subject to the coercion attempted by the Court of Session as above set forth; and that, at the risk and

hazard of suffering the loss of the secular benefits conferred by the State, and the public advantages of an Establishment, they must, as by God's grace they will, refuse so to do; for, highly as they estimate these, they cannot put them in competition with the inalienable liberties of a Church of Christ, which, alike by their duty and allegiance to their Head and King, and by their ordination vows, they are bound to maintain, 'notwithstanding of whatsoever trouble or persecution may arise.'

" ......and that, while they will accord full submission to all such acts and sentences, (e.g. Patronage Act and the sentences handed down by the courts) insofar - though insofar only - as these may regard civil rights and privileges, whatever may be their opinion of the justice or legality of the same, their said submission shall not be deemed an acquiescence therein....."

The relation of the Church to the State is a variation of the relation of the office-bearers to the decrees passed by the General Assembly of the Church in earlier days. The Patronage Act should be final but not absolute. The Church would not demand the removal of the Patronage Act immediately from the statute book. It would submit to the State so far as the ruling of the Patronage Act on temporalities was concerned. On the matter of conscience, there was an absolute refusal to submit, since in this matter, Christ's voice must alone have the pre-eminence.

The Church had made her point. Disobedience in 1842 was not to be considered insubordination, but submission to a higher call. In the Church's opinion, accommodation should be made for such a stance if the conditions of the Confession of Faith, which was itself a part of the statute law of the land were to be catered for. "The powers which God hath ordained," (in this case the government), "and the liberty which Christ hath purchased" (in this case exercised by the Evangelical majority), "are not intended by God to destroy, but mutually to uphold and preserve one another."

Separation came with the Protest of 1843. In 1843, it was the refusal of the Claim, Declaration and Protest and consequent admission to the Assembly of persons whose presence compromised the stance of the Evangelical majority that meant separation was inevitable. (The two protests of 1842 and 1843 give an indication of how different are protests against unlawful *acts* enacted by authorities whose lawfulness is not called into question, and protests against *authorities* which are protested against as being themselves constitutionally unlawful. In 1842, there was no question that the British Parliament was not a lawful assembly when it passed the Patronage Act in 1712, even though the Act itself was unlawful. The 1843 Protest was a protest against the Assembly, itself. "And we further protest, that any Assembly constituted in submission to the conditions now declared to be law, and under the civil coercion which has been brought to bear on the election of commissioners to the Assembly this day appointed to have been holden, and on the commissioners chosen thereto, is not and shall not be deemed a lawful and free Assembly of the Church of Scotland, according to the original and fundamental principles thereof". The former protest did not result in separation, since the Church had in view an arrangement by which the conscience of the Church would be satisfied. The latter did result in separation since the corollary of her claim that the Church of Scotland Assembly about to be convened was unlawful was that those who subscribed to the Claim Declaration and Protest of the previous Assembly made up the true Assembly of the Church of Scotland.

Fifty years later, the protests respectively in 1892 and 1893 can be seen in a similar light to those in 1842 and 1843. The Confession of Faith gave a summary of fundamental articles of belief drawn from the Scriptures. By substituting " 'the substance of the reformed faith' as contained in the Confession.....for the Confession itself, the Confession of Faith not only ceases to be the recognised standard of orthodoxy which it is at present, but the Church is left without any definite, fixed or authoritative standard of doctrine," (Reasons of Dissent of Constitutional Party). In going on to say that the Declaratory Act would not be binding upon them, the Constitutional Party were taking the same conscientious stance the emerging Free Church did in 1842 when it refused to administer the Patronage Act and left the State to consider how its scruples could be accommodated. This was not an act of separation. In receiving the Protest, the Assembly of 1892 acknowledges the right of the protesters to submit such a plea.

Mr Macfarlane's protest of 1893, by contrast, like the 1843 protest, was a protest against the Assembly. This Assembly, Mr Macfarlane asserts, now ceases to represent the Free Church. Commissioners who came declaring that they took office under the Declaratory Act could not be challenged. Any claim that the Protest of 1892 suspended the Declaratory Act was henceforth without substance. Commissioners would come, as I hope to show later, united not around the Confession as their common basis of belief, but around the substance of the faith. Separation for any who conscientiously signed the Protest of 1892 saying that the Declaratory Act was not binding upon them was inevitable as a consequence of the despotic overthrow of the protesting minority.

PART 3 -THE COLLAPSE OF THE HEAVENLIES.

CHAPTER 1

OUR SCIENTIFIC AGE

The following three chapters are, in one sense, somewhat of a diversion. They deal with the doctrinal background to the separation of the Free Presbyterian Church, and later the present Free Church from the Free Church of 1843. The basic reason for the separation, as noted in the second chapter, was the modifying of the creed of the (1843) Free Church so that instead of requiring subscription to the Confession of Faith as a whole, it required only subscription to the "substance of the reformed faith" contained in the Confession.

The reason for introducing this matter here is to show that there is a united witness that all three churches, Free Church, Free Presbyterian Church and Associated Presbyterian Church still have to display. All three churches have individual "family" concerns of their own, and hence the similarity in the witness is not given the prominence it might be given.

Creeds are like sea-walls. They keep out heresy. Most of the positions adopted in them were defined in times of pressure from heresy. When the sea has withdrawn to the foot of the wall, the wall itself may seem to be redundant. So, when there is vibrant spiritual life in the church, the need for protection from heresy slackens. When the sea is about to overwhelm the town, the sea-wall proves its worth. If breached at that time, subsequent generations will suffer.

This is illustrated in the century before the passage of the Declaratory Act. The late eighteenth century was a low point in Scottish spiritual history. Most of the lively witness of the times was to be found in the churches of dissent, the Original Secession and Relief churches. Taylor Innes in "Law of Creeds in Scotland", speculates that Dr Robertson, the leader of the Moderate Party retired from Assembly affairs prematurely because he was inundated with requests to change the Confession, which he was unwilling to do. He expected that after him would come the deluge. The deluge did not come, Taylor Innes thinks, at least partly because of the revival of religion in the early nineteenth century. As the doctrines of the Confession became meaningful again, so the pressure for reform receded. Had that pressure not been resisted in the eighteenth century, however, it would have been to the detriment of the church when revival did come.

In the late nineteenth century up to the present we are treated to an illustration of the same truths from the other side of the coin. The Confession of Faith was undermined and no replacement was put in position. The result is that in the Church of Scotland there is now, and has been for some time past, an acknowledgement that "the present law of the Church makes it very difficult to deal with any case in which a Minister or office-bearer is alleged to be holding or teaching doctrines contrary to the official belief of the Church. The reason for the difficulty is that, although the Westminster Confession is the chief subordinate standard of the Church, the terms in which Ministers and other office-bearers subscribe to it are so ill-defined that it is not easy to give them any precise meaning." (Report of the Panel of Doctrine, 1970). (The Church of Scotland adopted the same stance as the U.F. Church prior to union in 1929. This means that office-bearers subscribe to "the substance of the faith" contained in the Confession of Faith which was essentially the same stance as the Declaratory Act Free Church adopted in 1893.)

My aim in the subsequent chapters is to give some indication from whence came the underlying pressure for change in the Free Church of last century. When this has been described, it is easier to see what the united witness of the three churches referred to above should be.

Scripture is full of parables - earthly stories with heavenly meaning. One of these illustrates what I speak of as the "collapse of the heavenlies". Pharaoh dreamed a dream in Genesis 41. He saw seven "lean and ill-favoured" kine swallow up seven fat kine. When they had done this, "it could not be known that they had eaten them; but they were still ill-favoured as at the first." He saw seven ears of corn, "withered, thin, and blasted with the east wind" devour seven good ears, again without betterment.

The modern age is characterised by the knowledge explosion. That knowledge is knowledge by observation and experiment - we examine, we test we compare and contrast and we deduce the laws that govern the universe. Coupled with this, we have means to hand which enables us to expand immeasurably the information on which we can use our reason. Radio and optical telescopes plumb the depths of space, electron microscopes let us see down to the building-blocks of matter, to the molecules themselves. This to the typical modern man is knowledge. There is no other. Either consciously or unconsciously he accepts the verification principle, that when we cannot perceive anything by one or other of our senses, we cannot speak meaningfully about it.

For the believer, there is another kind of knowledge - knowledge which is there, but which because of our limited and finite capacities we will never be able to grasp. If you introduce an earthworm into the stock exchange, it will gain knowledge. It will be able to see light through a light-sensitive spot. It will be able to feel tremors. It will be conscious of the humidity of the air. Perhaps in some way it will be conscious of a continuous bustle around it the clatter of computers, the calling of the stock-brokers, the rush of feet back and forth. These things it does not have the equipment to understand. Hence, though it can claim to have the whole of knowledge so far as its own capacity to absorb that knowledge is concerned, and may go on increasing that knowledge, e.g. finding that it is more moist in a certain part of the space than another, or more bright near a window than in the centre of the room, it can never, because of its own limitations, know the whole, or even the real reason why the stock-exchange has been set up in the first instance.

God calls Jacob, (the people of Israel), a worm. (Is. 41;14). This is not in derision, but just for the same reasons we have mentioned. There are "secret things that belong to the Lord our God", and which none of us can ever know because we do not have the capacity. God dwells in "the light which no man can approach unto; whom no man hath seen, nor can see": I Tim 6:16. What makes man different from the worm in these circumstances is that he can know that he does not know. Socrates said he was the wisest of men precisely because of this reason, "he knew he did not know." Likewise, he can know that the appropriate response when he encounters what is beyond his understanding is not a curious enquiry, but the response of wonder. On the one hand he says, "How excellent is thy name in all the earth." On the other he says, "Lord, what is man, that thou art mindful of him?"

There is a third kind of knowledge, the knowledge of the open door. In moving on to this, the parable of the worm in the stock-exchange breaks down. One would have to think of the worm as having a real function in the stock exchange and having lost it, and only being able to re-discover that function by a renewed contact with the head of the stock exchange, itself. One would have to introduce a sense of wilful rebellion in the worm; that there are abilities which the worm does have, but wilfully does not use because the admission of the knowledge this information would lead to would interrupt the life-style he has chosen for himself. Just so, man has chosen "the creature rather than the Creator". He wants a world that he can dominate without being dominated. Hence, while there may be a general assent that God rules, the acknowledgement of the invisible power and sovereignty of God which presses on him from the witness of nature on all sides he leaves out of account so far as its practical effect on his day to day living is concerned. (Rom. 1; 19, 20). He is content to know about God, without knowing God himself. When Christ comes with a revelation of the love of God to a world in darkness, because one cannot receive the gifts of Christ without his lordship, "men love darkness rather than light, because their deeds were evil." Saul of Tarsus still "kicks against the pricks" even when the knowledge of the good news of salvation floods around him.

At this point, the heavenly door opened to Saul. "God who caused the light to shine out of darkness hath shined in our hearts, to give the light of the knowledge of the glory of God in the face of Jesus Christ." That day, he knew Christian liberty, and as a part of that Christian liberty, "access to God, not out of slavish fear, but a child-like love, and a willing mind." From that day, he had the power of private judgement. He knew what Isaiah meant when he spoke of being clothed with the garments of salvation and the robe of righteousness, because he had had the personal experience of a total disillusionment with his own righteousness. He had liberty of conscience to reject the whole baggage of Pharasaic righteousness and to reject any attempt to entrap him in the toils of such commandments of men he had once willingly obeyed.

The first knowledge, the knowledge of the world around us, can be there without the second, i.e. without belief in a higher spiritual and eternal world. Equally the second, nominal belief in a higher spiritual world in which God reigns supreme may be there without the third, the personal knowledge of God in "the face of Jesus

Christ." As a devout Pharisee, Paul believed in an invisible God so supreme and exalted that he could only be approached truly in the way of adoring worship; he believed in invisible spiritual beings such as angels and demons; he believed in unique spiritual power which was able even to resurrect the body. He believed man lived his true life in this heavenly realm, even while he was on earth. He would have wholly endorsed the words of Christ, "the life is more than meat and the body than raiment." Precisely the same God-believing outlook was a characteristic of the Middle Ages out of which Luther emerged, and he, himself, shared that outlook prior to his conversion.

What marks knowledge of the present day is that, like the thin ears of corn that swallowed up the fat ears, so knowledge that man has of the world around through the senses has swallowed up not only what is distinctive to the Christian revelation, but belief in the eternal world itself. By and large, "all that is" to the modern man is what he will eat, and drink and how he will be clothed, and all else is an irrelevance. Paul says that men are "earthly, sensual and develish." This to the typical modern man is meaningless. There is no other world than the earthly world, and to compare this world with a spiritual world leaves him incredulous. There are no other pleasures than those of sense. Hence, to speak of spiritual pleasure is equally meaningless. All that motivates him is his own thoughts and desires. To speak of being invaded by an alien spiritual being called the devil comes from the realm of fantasy. Such a world was left behind when we ceased to believe in dragons and witches and hobgoblins. And when the whole realm of the heavenlies is gone, it is pointless to speak of an open door either into it or from it.

To say that because the background to belief in a revelation from God, i.e. faith in God himself and in a heavenly realm, has gone, and therefore faith in specifically Christian truth has gone also, would be clearly wrong. Nevertheless, where that background is not there, the whole presuppositions of a Christian faith are ruled out of court at the same time. These presuppositions were already in Paul's mind when he met with Christ. He believed in a heavenly sphere, in the spiritual absolutes of truth, justice, love, holiness, in the finality of divine law and the judgement seat of God. It was in the *means* of attaining God's favour that his view was fundamentally changed when he met with Christ, not in belief that the search for the blessing of God's favour is the chief end of man. Now, when the reality of a heavenly sphere is at best an irrelevance, when a celebrated scientist like Richard Dawkins throws a tantrum, according to Bernard Levin, at the mere mention of God, all discussion associated with God's being, far less the seeking of His favour, is considered by the many as escapism from the realm of hard reality. The earth-worm really can, it is thought, understand all that goes on in the stock exchange. Only because he undervalues his own abilities and thinks the gaps in his knowledge are unassailable peaks he could never hope to scale does he fail to realise his own destiny. These gaps he attributes to the operation of some divine being. Science can fill these gaps, and the need for belief in God will disappear.

In the next chapter, I wish to show some indication of the collapse using writers of last century to illustrate aspects of it.

PART 3 - THE COLLAPSE OF THE HEAVENLIES.

CHAPTER 2

TRIBUTARIES OF UNBELIEF.

In the next two chapters, I hope to give an indication of how unbelief developed through the thought of the nineteenth century, and how it nurtured the kind of broad outlook which found expression in the Declaratory Act movement. The treatment is sketchy in the extreme, since this is not my main concern, but I trust it will at least give a background, however inadequate.

As mentioned in the last chapter, in the dream of Pharaoh interpreted by Joseph, there are five ears of corn, "blasted with the East Wind" who eat up the five good ears, and are no better. That's the kind of thing that many thinkers did in the 18th century. They swallowed up the whole theological realm, but did so, not to enrich their own perceptions, but to reduce that realm to nothing.

August Comte produced his "Positive Philosophy" between 1830 and 1842. Sciences were classed according to the decreasing simplicity and generality of their subject-matter - mathematics, astronomy, physics, chemistry, biology, and sociology. In each field of thought there had been a Law of Three Stages. First came theology when the subject had been explained in terms of the will of some deity. Second came the metaphysical stage, when ideas dreamed up in the mind of the metaphysician had taken over. Finally there was science, based on observation, hypothesis and experiment. Philosophy's aim was to co-ordinate all the sciences with a view to the improvement of human life. Where theology and metaphysics were trusted in without proceeding onward to the scientific stage, they led to a state of arrested development.

It is little wonder though Comte at the end of his life introduced a new religion of humanity with himself as high priest. That is the logical end of his thought. If our senses present us with the utmost limit of, not only knowledge as we may know it but of Knowledge as it is to be known by anyone, then man is God. The worm has become divine.

Comte is little read today, but "The Encyclopaedia Americana" regards his thought as "an important landmark in the development of modern scientific philosophy."

Around 1850, Marx was writing his "Das Capital". Spiritual things were dreams of the lower classes acting as compensation for their bitter lot. To dream that a Father in heaven cared for them, or that at the end of life's struggle, came the welcome of heaven, was natural for people doomed to spend their days in the Satanic mills of the Industrial Revolution. Comte had at least thought of the spiritual conception of things as an intermediate step to coming to reality. To Marx, religion was a pathological condition. In the perfect state, it would wither away.

I read once an account of a radio talk between Malcolm Muggeridge and Aneurin Bevan, the Socialist leader. As a representative of the far left, Bevan spoke as Marx would.   The subject of discussion was "The Pilgrim's Progress" by John Bunyan. The key to the story for Bevan was that John Bunyan was a tinker, travelling from village to village mending pots and pans.   As a member of an under-class, he lived in a City of Destruction.   His dream of the Celestial City was an unconscious dream of the proletariat for an egalitarian society, a projection of their dreams for justice, acknowledgement by worth and not by status, and freedom from capitalism.   The giants Christian met on the way to the Celestial City were representatives of moneyed monsters who must forcibly be fought, ("You don't make omelettes without cracking eggs"), and overcome.

Without doubt, socialism can be separated as a political idea from religion.   Nevertheless, on the construction of Marx, God was ruled out.   It is little wonder that Moscow had a temple to atheism during the Communist rule.

Evolution as a theory had a long history.   Evolution which made struggle followed by the survival of the fittest its key came with Charles Darwin in the 1860s.   For the atheistic evolutionist, God was the god of the gaps.   There had been gaps in men's understanding.   How did the world come into being?   How did higher and higher life-forms arise?   As "phlogiston" was invented to explain combustion because men knew no better; as "caloric" was invented to explain heat; as "ether" was invented because it was unimaginable that space could be empty;   so, God had been invented as an over-all invisible and equally ineffable fountain of life to explain the origin of all things in general and each in particular.   This is not to say that Darwin, himself, expresses himself thus.   However men such as Thomas Huxley found in "The Origin of Species" freedom, as he thought, from the need to look higher than the operations of the natural world to explain life in all its diversity.

> "The "Origin" provided us with the working hypothesis we sought. Moreover it did the immense service of freeing us for ever from the dilemma - Refuse to accept the Creation hypothesis, and what have you to propose that can be accepted by any cautious reasoner? In 1857, I had no answer, and I do not think anyone else had. A year later, we reproached ourselves with dulness."

Why was it so desirable to eject the view of creation? Creation carries with it the vision of a transcendent Being who inhabits a transcendent sphere who speaks and it is done. Such a sphere represents to man what the stock exchange does to the worm; it is an area into which he cannot enter. It is an area which we cannot lay on the slab of man's reason to be dismembered and dissected at his will. The ground on which he stands is holy, and the only appropriate response its to take the shoes from one's feet. Seeing life as the impact of time on matter bringing life into being, and then the further development of life as due to minute variations leading to a greater chance of survival for those who have favourable changes liberated the scientist from coming face to face with any divine superintendance at all.

Herbert Spencer was as much struck with the evolutionary idea as Huxley, and used it to take a broad survey of human development. Men are what their environment makes them, in his view. There is no heavenly calling since there are no heavens. The great development in sociology was not to be expected from religious conversion, since men were the product of their environment. It was taking place as men turned from war to industrial pursuits.

The warrior state was centralised and authoritarian. It worshipped a warrior god. It developed class distinctions. As industry became widespread, so would democracy and peace. Not only foreign war but domestic brutality would decrease. Religions with superstitious views would yield to creeds which in liberal fashion would strive for the ennoblement and amelioration of life on this side of the grave.

Like Comte, Spencer is little read today, but in his own time his books were used as texts in Oxford University.

Freud sought to exorcise religion not merely from the state or from man's conception of the development of life but from the soul, itself. He ponders the problem why there should be three elements which he isolates in religion. There is view of God as creator, as the consoler and as the one who gives ethical commands. Psycho-analysis, Freud assures us, reveals that this being, (God), is really the image of the father, "clothed in the grandeur in which he once appeared to the small child. The religious man's picture of the creation of the universe is the same as his picture of his own creation." (New Introductory Lectures on Psycho-analysis).
God, in other words, is a projection flowing out of our earliest impressions.

To each one of these men, contemporary religious orthodoxy of the worship of a being "dwelling in light inaccessible and full of glory", was not a sign of maturity, but of either stunted development or escapism. It was an evidence of inadequacy within man, himself, either inadequacy, with Freud, of understanding the workings of his own mind, or with Comte of the universe or with Darwin in his illustration of his dog barking at a flapping parasol of comprehension that though there may seem to be supernatural powers at work, these powers are, in fact, natural in origin. Man, in superstitious guise, invests them with supernatural dignity. Let man once dare to use his reason to its full potential, and no barrier will stand in his way.

Freud, ("Civilisation and its Discontents"), having listed man's achievements in inventing machinery, telescopes, the camera, the telephone, etc., says, "It sounds like a fairy-tale, but not only that: this story of what man by his science and practical inventions has achieved on this earth, where he first appeared as a weakly member of the animal kingdom ,... is a direct fulfilment of all or of most, of the dearest wishes of his fairy-tales. All these possessions he has acquired through culture. Long ago, he acquired an ideal conception of omnipotence and omniscience which he embodied in his gods. Whatever seemed unattainable to his desires - or forbidden to him, he attributed to these gods. One may say, therefore, that these gods were the ideals of his culture. Now he has himself approached very near to realising this ideal, he has nearly become a god, himself. ... Future ages will produce further great advances in this realm of culture, probably inconceivable now, and will increase man's likeness to a god still more."

The common man whether he read such writers as the above or not, was by and large coming to the same conclusions. There was such a gigantic leap forward in man's achievements, as Freud notes, that Comte's dream of the divinity of man, or Neitsche's claim that God was dead seemed to have more than a grain of truth to support it. Britain was expanding its imperial power in the far east. In the 1850s it had pushed its conquests in India up to the Himalayas. The world was fast becoming a "global village". Japan was coming out of its isolation and decreed in 1868 that knowledge should be sought all over the world. The Industrial Revolution continued its advance. Sewing machines were patented, reapers developed, steam turbines provided power, first gas and then electricity brought cheap power into the home, precision tools made possible mass production, and in the field of communications, cheaper newspapers and magazines brought information to a wider readership. Great engineering projects like the Caledonian Canal early in the century, and the Forth Road Bridge and the Eiffel Tower later showed man's ability to tame Nature. On land, Stevenson's "Rocket" made possible rapid access to the furthest regions when once the great rail-building programme had been completed. On sea, Cunard began their trans-Atlantic service in 1840. For those who could not wait to make the journey and meet their contact face to face, there emerged the ideal answer in 1876. Then Alexander Graham Bell held his first telephone conversation.

It was easy to think that the great advance in material terms was equivalent to an equal advance in the real state of humanity. Henry Adams in visiting the Paris Exposition in 1900 said, "Man has translated himself into a new universe which has no common scale of measurement with the old." The basis of this new universe was confidence in man's intellect and courage in the exercise of it. As this helter skelter of progress rushed onwards, few had the reflectiveness of mind to say with John Morely, "as we sing hymns of triumph, to commerce, to the speed of a trading race over the globe, we are deaf and blind to the cost of so much glory, and forget how little it all adds to the moral stature of men." More were echoing the words of Matthew Arnold,

> The Sea of faith
> Was once, too, at the full, and round earth's shore
> Lay like the folds of a bright girdle furl'd.
> But now I only hear
> Its melancholy, long withdrawing roar,
> Retreating, to the breath
> Of the night wind, down the vast edges drear
> And naked shingles of the world.

PART 3: THE COLLAPSE OF THE HEAVENLIES

CHAPTER 3

RECIPIENTS AND DISPENSERS OF UNBELIEF.

In 1880 there appeared a volume with the uninspiring title of "Scotch Sermons". The thirteen contributors were of the more avant-garde ministers in the Church of Scotland, but the fact that it was sermons they published and not essays tucked away in some theological journal, showed they considered this teaching to be meat for the masses. A sample may be taken from Rev. W.L. M'Farlan, Lenzie. The text is, "That the things that cannot be shaken may remain."

Mr M'Farlane begins, "That the old theologies are being shaken by the new sciences is a fact which is patent to the most superficial observation. .... To what extent, we have to enquire, do such religious teachers admit that the old beliefs in which they were indoctrinated are endangered by the new theories which, it is alleged, must supersede them entirely? They admit, we may venture to reply for them, that insofar as these beliefs were embodied in the dogmas of scholastic theology, they must be abandoned or greatly modified. The sections of that theology which treat of sin and salvation they regard as specially untenable. These sections comprehend the following dogmas: (1) the descent of man from the Adam of the Book of Genesis; (2) the fall of that Adam, from a state of original righteousness, by eating the forbidden fruit; (3) the imputation of Adam's guilt to all his posterity; (4) the consequent death of all men in sin; (5) the redemption in Christ of an election according to grace; (6) the quickening in the elect of a new life - (a) at their baptism, Catholics affirm - (b) at the moment of their conversion, most Protestants allege; (7) the eternal punishment and perdition of those who remain unregenerate. These sections of the traditional theology of Christendom, - originally elaborated by Augustine, amended and developed by the schoolmen of the Middle Ages, adopted wholesale by the Puritans, - dominated the Christian intellect for centuries. They have ceased to dominate it. They no longer press on the minds and spirits of men like an incubus."

The message of the scientist is now the message of the pulpit. Election implies dependance on another.   Man is now so thoroughly independent, that he need not show such weakness. Man must walk tall.   The redemption of Christ is not only dispensable; it is inadmissible.   Equally inadmissible is the application of redemption to man in the quickening of the elect to new life. "Ever since the Reformation", Mr M'Farlan goes on to say, "the spirit of free enquiry has been destroying, bit by bit, the structure of scholastic theology.   During the last quarter of a century, she has been attacking it with hands more than ever bold and busy.   In consequence of her attacks, the ancient structure is now tottering to its fall."

Every one of the doctrines condemned by Mr M'Farlan are to be found, not in Augustine as their fountain-head, nor in the scholastic theologians, but in Holy Scripture.   That is not mentioned for the obvious reason that Augustine and the scholastic theologian could be attacked as men that had "sprung of earth." Among the masses, at least, there was still enough reverence around for the Word of God as Divine truth that attack on these doctrines as contained in Scripture would have recoiled upon the attacker.

Comte's religion of man has all but invaded the church. There is no need any more to wait patiently on God till He inclines his ear to our cry. Our imperfections themselves are so many steps by which we may rise to higher worlds. "The sense of sin", says Mcfarlan, "impels man to long and strive for better things." The Fall is a fall upward.

It is fair to say that in the 1881 Assembly, Robert Flint insisted that Mr Macfarlan give satisfaction of his allegiance to the fundamental doctrines of the faith. The next day he gave an apology. It is also fair to ask which represented the true views of Mr Macfarlane, and which would have had the more abiding impression - an apology which must have passed in a matter of minutes, and which would have come to the notice of but a few, or the sermons with their reasoned arguments which remained on men's shelves influencing opinion throughout the country.

It might have been thought that the strong evangelical bias of the Free Church would have saved her from invasion by views of this nature. Long before the latter part of the century, there were evidences of the influence of more liberal views. I will confine myself to two professors who were teaching at the time of the introduction of the Declaratory Act, A.B. Bruce and Marcus Dodds. The former was Professor of Apologetics and New Testament Exegesis in the FC Divinity Hall in Glasgow from 1875. The latter was appointed Professor of New Testament Criticism and Exegesis in 1889 in New College, Edinburgh.

I will first examine an argument used by Dr Dodds for jettisoning the Confessional view of the limits of Scripture. Having seen where this leads, I hope to go on to see how Prof. Bruce uses these principles to find the true essence of Scripture doctrine.

On 15th November, 1891, Dr Dodds addressed a meeting of the Young Men's Christian Association in Edinburgh. These are the words in which he spoke of the canon of Scripture - that was the subject of the talk which was given - and the way in which the canon was dealt with in the creeds of the Church. (The Westminster Confession simply details the books of the Bible and says of the whole list, "All which are given by inspiration of God, to be the rule of faith and life.")

"When the well-authenticated writings of such persons (i.e. persons authorised by Christ to give His truth to the world) came into their hands, they accepted them if they were already Christians; but then, there were books in the Bible whose inspiration could not be ascertained by either of these methods. Chronicles, Esther, Job, Ecclesiastes - no one knew who wrote these books. One of the methods of ascertaining inspiration was therefore closed, and as to the inward witness, he was not persuaded that the book of Esther could have been accepted as an inspired book had it been found outside the Jewish Canon. From all this they might gather, first - the Churches should be cautious in speaking of the canon as an absolute definite collection of writings, thoroughly and to a nicety ascertained, based on definite principles, and precisely separated at every point from all extra-canonical literature. There was no reasonable doubt that the bulk of the books of the New Testament came so accredited that to reject them was equivalent to rejecting the authority of Christ; but a few were not so accredited; and it was a question whether our creeds ought not to reflect the fact that in the early Church some books were universally admitted into the Canon while regarding seven of the books of the New Testament grave doubts are entertained."

Dr Dodds brings in a new foundation of authority.

"Let them always remember that the true Protestant order was, first, faith in Christ; and second, faith in Scripture. Their faith in Christ did not hang upon their faith in Scripture as an inspired Book, but their faith in Scripture hung upon their faith in Christ. He and he only was the true Protestant who knew that God had spoken to him in Christ, and he knew this irrespective of any infallible authority separate from Christ himself, whether it were the authority of a Church, or the authority of Scripture."

All this has a strong spiritual ring to it. The Ethiopian in Acts does, indeed, come to the knowledge of Christ through the 53rd chapter of Isaiah, but he goes on his way rejoicing, not in the bare fact that the exegesis of the chapter has been explained to him by Philip, but because he has now met that Christ for himself. Now, Dr Dodds will claim, he will know that that chapter in Isaiah is inspired because there he met Christ.

The great weakness of this position is that we have now moved from an objective standard - the Scriptures from Genesis to Revelation - to a subjective standard - our experience of Christ through the Scriptures. Can we be sure that the Christ whom we have met is the real Christ?

In 1892, Prof. Bruce published his "Apologetics". Dr Bruce's statements are particularly of interest since he was summoned before the Free Church Assembly in 1890 to answer for statements in earlier books, "The Miraculous Elements in the Gospels", and "The Kingdom of God" in which he denied the Gospel accounts were free from error.   When the book on apologetics came out, Mr Macaskill, Dingwall, tried to raise objections before the College committee. He was unsuccessful. Hence, we may regard the views expressed in the "Apologetics" as typical of the kind of views which, if they were tolerated in the Free Church before the Declaratory Act had been passed, though not without opposition, could be freely stated without challenge thereafter.

So far as the importance of Christ is concerned, Dr Bruce takes exactly the same stance as Dr Dodds in saying that first there must be faith in Christ and only then faith in the Scriptures.

> "For one   section of Christendom (the RCs), the
> Church has taken his place as Lord, for another, (the
> Protestants), the Bible; in either case without
> intention, and for the most part without consciousness
> of disloyalty. The question as to the seat of authority
> is sometimes formulated without reference to Christ,
> the only alternatives thought of being the Bible, the
> church or reason.   In view of such facts, it is
> incumbent to resurrectionise the buried commonplace
> and to reassert with emphasis that Jesus Christ is the
> Lord of Christendom, and the Light of the World."

At least Dr Dods does say that to reject the bulk of the books of the New Testament was equivalent to rejecting the authority of Christ. That, surely would give the assurance that at the very least those historical books which recount Christ's life on earth would be considered authoritative. One finds that even this stance of Dr Dodds is unceremoniously blown away by Dr

Bruce. The following is the way in which Dr Bruce speaks of the writing of the Gospel of John:

> "We cannot but feel that one who could remember dates and places, and even the very hour of the day at which particular incidents occurred, could equally well recall words, unless there were some other influence at work causing them to disappear from consciousness. Such an influence we may discover in the transmuting activity of the Evangelist's mind acting upon the original data, the words of the Lord Jesus....and as the tree is potentially in the seed, so a devoted disciple may feel that the whole system of thought, which has grown up in his mind out of the germs of truth deposited there by his Master may be - nay ought to be - accredited to that Master. He may therefore deem it quite unnecessary anxiously to distinguish between what the Master actually said, and what grew out of it."

The whole system of thought in John's gospel, then, may be a graft that John has imposed on the original thought of Christ, and owe nothing to Christ, Himself. There are two ways in which such a passage reflects not only on John but on Christ Himself. The reason why apostolic accreditation was thought so important was that Christ had explicitly said that the Spirit would bring all things to their remembrance, whatsoever He had said to them. If John in writing his epistle was, in reality, left to the musings of his own heart, then his views have even less authority than that views of the most casual hearer of Christ who faithfully set down what he had heard directly after he had heard it. If John was merely a dreamer who transformed the original, we cannot know what that original was.

The second way in which this passage reflects on Christ is in taking all real mystery out of his life and ministry, and substituting a complete mystification. Clearly, Dr Bruce is referring to the places where John says Christ claimed for Himself a place entirely unique. "I and the Father are one." He is the "Son of man who is in heaven." John is not alone in making claims like this for Christ, ("....neither knoweth any man the Father save the Son, and he to whomsoever the Son will reveal him." Matthew 11;27) For the reader in the 19th century, the pressing question is, "Is there a living, divine Christ who can open the door of grace for me?"

It is the reality of the resurrection, and seeing the death of Christ in the light of that resurrection, that filled the hearts of the disciples with joy. Yet when we turn to Dr. Bruce's estimation of the resurrection we are sorely disappointed. He speaks of Strauss who pledges himself to show that there could be a "belief in the resurrection without any corresponding miraculous fact." Instead of condemning such a view, Bruce says, "Whatever diversity of opinion may prevail as to the importance of the historic fact, there is entire agreement as to the vital importance of the *belief* (his italics) in the fact entertained by the apostles and the Church founded by them."

By this time a pattern seems clearly to emerge in the way Dr. Bruce deals with the life of Christ. Where there is any indication of suggestion of divine, supernatural action, it is played down.

> "We have been too much accustomed," says Bruce "to talk about Christ's Messianic claims, without being sufficiently sensitive lest we should appear to make Him appear to be animated by ambitious passions or by vain self-importance. We must be careful so to state his attitude towards His Messianic vocation that these unholy elements shall be eliminated. This is possible by looking on the

> Messiahship on the side of duty rather than on the
> side of dignity, and by giving prominence to the
> suffering aspect of the Messiah's career."

The simple way in which it can be made evident that Christ was
not boastful in making Messianic claims is by showing Christ
was the Messiah, and the Messiah, rightfully, could claim to be
divine.

There was an emperor once who was so depressed by a particular
desolate part of his empire that he had a facade constructed of
houses along the route he must follow when passing through this
region. In spite of the colourful and lively appearance on the
outside, the doors led through only to a barren desert.

If the concept of "Logos", for instance, which John used to
describe Christ were only one found in the current Greek thought
and was used by him to apply to Christ; if, at the same time, it
would have been "vain self-importance" for Christ, Himself, to
have used such a title, with all the divine attributes associated
with it; then all the qualities that are depicted by the Logos as
the Word of God are only an empty facade; in particular, the
door that Christ claims to be to the Father is only a figment of the
imagination, and reliance on Christ as such a door can only lead
to disillusionment in the end.

John claims in his first epistle that Christ was still in living
fellowship with him, ("Truly our fellowship is with the Father
and with His Son, Jesus Christ", 1 John 1;3). According to the
above construction, John was in fellowship only with a creature
of his own imagination. Indeed, the whole of John's message to
us crumbles to dust, since he himself ceases to be credible. No
longer is that message, "These things are written unto you that ye
might believe that Jesus is the Son of God, and that believing ye
might have life through His name." It becomes, "These things
are written that ye might believe that John inflates the character

of Christ to unreal and unbelievable proportions, and believing this might congratulate yourselves on your critical acumen in detecting the imposition." The aim of Dr Bruce is to deflect the criticism that he sees a scientific age will heap on what they regard such an unreal figure. The question is, once one has so levelled down Christ, what is there left worth believing in? If ever there was a twilight figure, it is here. This is all the more distressing that Bruce makes the figure of Christ the great foundation of faith as quoted above, when he speaks of Jesus Christ as "the Lord of Christendom, and the light of the world." What wonderful sentiments; but when one finds that the very characteristics in Christ which led the Early Church to call Jesus, "Lord", his lordship over a creation He Himself brought into being, and His lordship as the resurrected Lamb in the midst of the throne seem to be considered dispensable, is it any wonder one feels like the dove who found no place for the sole of her foot.

It is not Christ that is lord here. It is not the Church. It is not the Scriptures. The answer peeps out on every page. It is human reason. There are drawbacks about the thought of creation. "How was God occupied before he created the world?" The fall of man is brought into line with ideas of evolution. Man has a higher and a lower nature. ,The higher is human, the lower is animal. Perhaps it would be enough to quote "The Freethinker" of January 29, 1893.

> "What has it" (i.e. Christianity), "always meant? Belief in the deity of Christ, his absolute authority as a teacher, his atonement for the sins of believers, future rewards and punishments, salvation by faith, the depravity of human nature, the efficacy of prayer, the inspiration of the Bible, the revealed will of God, as the rule and sanction of morality..... Now if this be Christianity, it is undoubtedly played out. Of course, I may be accused of writing as a partisan. Well, I ask anyone to read an old standard book like "Pearson on

the Creed", and then a new book like Professor Bruce's "Apologetics", and I am much mistaken if he will not feel that Christianity is in the last state of nebulosity."

In 1890, Prof. Bruce had been summoned before the General Assembly to answer for some of his statements. The decision of the Assembly was that while some of his statements had been unguarded, his teachings were not in breach of the Westminster Confession. Rev. Murdo MacAskill, Dingwall, as noted above, tried to have some action taken against Prof. Bruce for his book, "Apologetics", through the College Committee, but failed.

It is clear that if the figure of Christ painted by Dr Bruce is a misty figure, his view of Scripture will be correspondingly misty. It is through Christ we are to come to Scripture. When we arrive at Christ we are only half-way there. If a reliable assessment of the claims of Christ is totally dependent on our judgement of whether the evangelists - who, after all, were immeasurably nearer the Christ they wrote of than we are - are telling the truth, then every man must make his own Christ, and every man must make his own Scriptures, selecting the passages that meet his own preconceptions, and rejecting others.

The toleration of such views within the Free Church was bad enough. At the same time, the fact that the Free Church held onto the Westminster Confession of Faith as its touchstone of orthodoxy, meant that all office-bearers must sign the Confession of Faith as the confession of their faith. In 1892, this would change. In that year, a Declaratory Act would be passed which would call for subscription only to "the substance of the reformed faith in the Confession." This would mean one could virtually make one's confession as a tailor makes a suit according to his cloth.

Luther drew up a series of theses against rationalism before he drew up his these against indulgences. He found no-one to debate with him these theses. Yet throughout his writings his attitude to reason is clear.

> "Luther often railed at reason, and he has been portrayed in consequence as a complete irrationalist in religion. This is quite to mistake his meaning. Reason in the sense of logic he employed to the uttermost limits. At Worms, and often elsewhere, he asked to be instructed from Scripture and reason. In this sense, reason meant logical deduction from known premises; and when Luther railed against the harlot reason, he meant something else. Common sense is perhaps a better translation. He had in mind the way in which man ordinarly behaves, feels and thinks. It is not what God says that is a foreign tongue, but what God does that is utterly incomprehensible," (Bainton pp. 172-173).

Whether man adds to (Indulgences, Bodily Assumption of Mary, Virtue of Relics etc.) or, applying the acid of his own sceptical criticism, subtracts from the testimony of Scripture, the challenge of the upholder of the veracity of Scripture is the same. Is the voice of a God whose ways and thoughts are above ours as the heavens are above the earth to be heard in reverential silence? The premises from which Luther began was the testimony of the Scriptures. Adding or subtracting from the Word of God had the same effect. God's voice is mingled with man's and loses its power.

At the same time, it can be said that the one who subtracts is more dangerous. When a person adds to the Bible, his additions stand out in bold relief. When a person subtracts, it is usually by investing already established language with new meaning. As a result, the person can say, "Jesus is Lord", and mean no more than that the teaching of Christ gives him a unique place among the prophets of the ages. He can recite these words along with the traditionally orthodox, but the words are poetry rather then sober truth.

What unites the three churches, Free Church, Free Presbyterian, and Associated Presbyterian Churches is that they believe not merely in the authority of the original witness - the various ways in which God at sundry times spoke in times past to our fathers through the prophets, and has in time past spoken unto us by His Son. They believe in the authority of the medium by which that revelation has come down to us. Hence, they do not speak merely of Scripture pointing past itself to Christ. All Scripture is itself authoritative since inspired by God. When we are told that we need not ascend to heaven to bring Christ down from above, or descend into the deep to bring up Christ from below since the word is nigh us, we can believe that as truly as Jacob found the gate of heaven where he was in the desert, so may we. When the liberal theologian hears of Christ in the word of God, it is a signal for him mount an expedition to find that Christ, armed with his critical acumen, since the Word of God is only a witness to a past revelation. That past revelation he feels at liberty to handle freely. It is but a short step from this point to the position of Feuerbach, who learnt from Schliermacher, the father of Liberal theology, and who said, "God is himself the realised wish of the heart, the wish exalted to the certainty of fulfilment....the secret of theology is nothing else than anthropology - the knowledge of God nothing else than the knowledge of man." Full-blown secular humanism is just round the corner.

PART 4: JUBILEE WITHOUT CHEER

CHAPTER 1

DR RAINY OF EDINBURGH AND SCOTLAND

I have entitled this section "Jubilee without Cheer" since, in the first place, 1893 was, indeed, the Jubilee of the Free Church.

It was without cheer, not because she was not now acknowledged world-wide, a fact that was seen in the series of deputations which came to the General Assembly in 1893 to give fulsome praise to her in recognition of her stance for truth. Moreover, she had become a sanctuary, first for large sections of the Original Secession Church, and then for the Reformed Presbyterians. It was without cheer because in 1893 the reverse tendency revealed itself. The Free Church through the introduction of the Declaratory Act could no longer provide a home to some of the most faithful of her followers. Neither to those who remained, nor to those who departed, could this have been any source of comfort. At the centre of the move for change, though not by any means the most zealous promoter of it, was Dr Rainy, who guided affairs in the Assembly. He felt the pulse for change and responded.

Dr Rainy was a man with a mission, and the accomplishment of that mission was the more imperative that it had been frustrated once before.

Coincidentally, the number "3" seems to recur in the history of the Free Church last century. In 1833 the Evangelical section of the Church of Scotland - destined to be the basis of the Free Church when separation came ten years later - gained a majority in the General Assembly.

In 1843, thwarted in its efforts first to minimise the evils of patronage, and then to have it abolished altogether, the evangelical section left to form the Church of Scotland, Free.

In 1863 preliminary moves were made to sound out the possibility of union between the Free Church and the other large, non-established presbyterian church, the United Presbyterian Church. After a promising beginning, negotiations foundered.

In 1873 they were terminated.

Two things had happened in the intervening interval. The Free Church had been split, internally, in two. One section which became known as the Constitutional Party, sounded the alarm that if the union had gone ahead, vital parts of the witness of the Free Church would have been lost. That section was led by Dr. Begg. From that time onward they appointed themselves the guardians of the unadulterated reformed witness which the Free Church claimed to uphold. The second thing that happened was that Dr Rainy emerged as the clear leader of the majority party.

Attempts at union failed, not because Dr Rainy could not command a sufficient majority in the General Assembly, but because of the extreme lengths the Constitutional Party were willing to go to thwart his purpose. It was made abundantly clear that the Constitutional Party which emerged during the struggle would separate if union went ahead. Was it worthwhile healing one split, that between the UP and FC, only to open up another? Dr Rainy called Dr Begg's party "the desperadoes", but desperadoes or not, Dr Rainy had to submit. Negotiations were shelved.

Various views have been expressed as to the motivation of Dr Rainy in desiring to effect this union. Alasdair Philips, the Glasgow Herald columnist, doubtless echoing the views of his uncle, Rev. George Mackay, describes his aims thus: Dr Rainy, he thought, "hankered after the larger empire he might command by uniting his 1,068 congregations with the United Presbyterians' 593."

It is not surprising though Dr Carnegie Simpson, the author of Dr Rainy's biography, takes a more sympathetic view. He sees Dr Rainy rather as the voice of the Free Church seeking to eliminate the blot of unnecessary divisions from the Church of Christ. This was an object all the more desirable, as he judged the Free Church at fault in drawing back in 1873. Dr Simpson quotes a letter written in 1889 to Dr Thomson, one of the leaders in the United Presbyterian Church.

> "The suspension of action on the part of our church in 1873 left us looking forward to union with your Church as the event hoped for in the future, though for the present set aside. I think it my duty - and the more pressing duty as the years pass - to take opportunity for making it plain that we maintain that attitude, that we realise the evils of indefinite delay, and especially that we feel an obligation resting on the Free Church in the matter which concerns her public character."

How this vision is viewed is immaterial. It may be seen in terms of naked ambition. It may be thought of as zeal for the elimination of unnecessary division from the face of Christ's kirk in Scotland. At the highest level, it may be thought of as the aim of a man so wrapped up in the will of Christ that he could write in the 1863-73 debate, "The Church of Christ has no liberty to become a slave even of its own history. History is great, but Christ is greater." For our purposes, it is necessary only to show that, as the above letter evidences, Dr Rainy was straining at the leash. Efforts to bring a union to fruition were "more pressing as the years pass."

When such a mission is found in such a man, it could mean only one thing. Action would be forthcoming.

Dr Rainy combined an inner daring with an outward restraint, even suavity. Both are illustrated in an early incident at the age of ten. He was sliding down banisters on his chest when he lost his balance, and fell twenty feet. His father heard the crash, and thought he might have been killed. He rushed to the spot, to be greeted by his son; "I beg your pardon, sir; I'll never do it again."

The daring was illustrated to more serious intent when Dean Stanley, Dean of Westminster, visited Edinburgh in 1872 to give a series of lectures purporting to show that covenanters, seceders, and disruptionists had been men of such scrupulosity that they could not see the really broad issues that were of truly lasting significance. It was the moderates, those very moderates who opposed the Evangelicals from whom the Free Church sprang, who provided the best tradition of the Church of Scotland. "The general theological and ecclesiastical conclusion," says Carnegie Simpson, "was that the bright future of Scottish religion would be to rally around a national Church which would be 'moderate' in manners and indeterminate in dogma and of course Erastian in policy."

Dean Stanley's last lecture was delivered on the 12th of January. Dr Rainy gave these lectures in reply on the 24th, 26th and 31st of the same month. "There is general admiration of the pluck which our champion has shown in being ready within ten days," wrote Dr McLagan to Dr Buchanan.

Without doubt, Dr Rainy did not lack spirit. The Constitutionalists feared the lack might lie in other directions, and the fact that Dr Rainy did not lack mettle only made that concern the greater.

The restraint and suavity developed in the courts of the Church into a kind of typical "Rainy-speak". One can almost feel the antennae of Dr Rainy's sensitivity to the convictions of those to whom he speaks reaching out assessing each tremor, and adjusting accordingly. Consider, for instance, a quotation given by Dr Carnegie Simpson, his biographer, on Dr Rainy's views on the inspriation of Scripture; "Personally, he held, or was inclined to hold, though he did it under difficulties, and he did not find the difficulties in holding it decreasing, that they might find, after all, that God had preserved the Scriptures, even in minor matters, from real error." ("The Life of Dr Rainy", vol. 2, p. 113.) Each section of the church might find satisfaction - or otherwise - in this statement. The believer in plenary inspiration could cite his statement that he thought the Scriptures free from real error, the man who has begun to doubt the fact he holds this under difficulties, and the man who is far down-stream that these difficulties are increasing, and hence before long, Dr Rainy will have arrived at his own stance. Under the convolution of the language, and the checks and counter-checks, ("*inclined to* hold", "*real* error"), it is practically impossible to know exactly where Dr Rainy stands.

The United Presbyterian Church had not made prospects of a successful union any more easy by a Declaratory Act which they passed in 1879. One of the principal difficulties which had figured in the 1863-73 debate was the relation of the United Presbyterian Church to Church establishment. Neither Free

Church nor United Presbyterian were established. The difference lay in the fact that the Free Church, on principle, supported the concept of establishment, and the United Presbyterian Church opposed it. Church establishment had been the most serious difficulty in the union debates in the years, 1863-73. The 1879 Act introduced a further difficulty. Liberty of opinion was now to be allowed on such points in the standards as did not enter into the substance of the faith. Office-bearers were free to avail themselves of the relaxation provided by this new stance, as was made clear in the formula subscribed by them: "Do you confess the Westminster Confession of Faith and the Larger and Shorter Catechisms as an exhibition of the sense in which you understand the Holy Scriptures, this acknowledgement being made in view of the explanations contained in the Declaratory Act of Synod thereanent?"

Like a computer virus, as we have already noticed, the phrase, "the substance of the faith," has spread itself from the Free Church to the United Free and then into the Church of Scotland. The corresponding question put to probationers when being called to a congregation in the Free Church was uncompromising in its call for loyalty to the whole of Confessional doctrine: "Do you sincerely own and believe the whole doctrine contained in the Confession of Faith, approven by former General Assemblies of this Church to be founded on the word of God; and do you acknowledge the same as the confession of your faith?" A person who subscribed to this could not, it seemed, subscribe with any degree of honesty to the UP questions and formula. With the difference in subscription introduced by the UP 1879 Act, it seemed an unbridgeable chasm had been opened up between the two Churches.

Union between the Free Church and the United Presbyterian could not be contemplated till such a disparity of views had been reconciled. As a result, the Free Church Declaratory Act was spawned.

In 1889, the year in which the above letter was written to Dr Thomson of the United Presbyterian Church, a committee was set up under the joint convenorship of Dr Rainy and a Dr Adam, with the aim of bringing about modification to the subscription to the Confession of Faith. Dr Adam died a little more than a year after, and Dr Rainy thereafter became sole convenor.

In a speech to the Assembly, Dr Rainy suggested three alternatives. The United Presbyterian Church example might be followed, and a Declaratory Act introduced. A more radical solution would be the adoption of a smaller Confession which would take the place of the old. A third possibility could be the changing of the questions and formula.

It was hardly surprising that the first alternative was adopted. This was exactly the line set by the United Presbyterian precedent. It was also hardly surprising that virtually the same phraseology was adopted in relaxing the terms of subscription to the Confession of Faith as had been adopted in the UP Church ten years before. The United Presbyterian Church had called for adherence to "the substance of the faith." The Free Church added one word. It called for adherence to "the substance of the reformed faith". In essence there was nothing to choose between them.

In 1891, Principal Rainy brought forward the Act it was proposed to place before the Assembly. A motion to adopt the Act passed by 428 to 66. In 1892, having been examined and approved by a majority of presbyteries, the Act became law.

A major hurdle on the way to the accomplishment of Dr Rainy's purpose had been surmounted; or had it?

There remained two difficulties. The Declaratory Act of the United Presbyterian Church was explicitly acknowledged in the formula signed and the questions put to candidates for the ministry in that Church. The Questions and Formula in the Free Church still, it would seem, bound the candidate uncompromisingly to the Confession of Faith in its totality. How, then, could any Free Church office-bearer avail himself of the new Act?

The second difficulty had to do with the Constitutional minority. The Act stated that the new views were the views of the Church. By 1892, when passed by the consent of presbyteries, these views had become binding laws and constitutions. Yet the prologue of the Act was almost apologetic about the imposition of such views on all and sundry.

> "Whereas it is expedient to remove difficulties and scruples which have been felt by some in reference to the declaration of belief required from persons who receive licence or are admitted to office in this Church, the General Assembly, with consent of Presbyteries, declare as follows:-"

Admission is freely made that only some required the relaxation. When that relaxation became binding, what of the consciences of those who heartily rejected the relaxation. Where were they to find relief?

Dr Rainy was at his most expansive in his acknowledgement of the difficulties of the minority.

In 1892 he says,

> "Now, I am very far from disregarding the dissent that has been expressed on this subject; and if this Act were an act proposing to lay fresh obligations, specific obligations on the minds of our office-bearers - either within the Church or about to enter it - if it

were to lay some now Confessional burden upon
them, I should regard the dissent of much less than 23
Presbyteries as a very strong reason for halting and
considering where we stand. But this Act will never
be used in this way. As to the precise terms in which
the Church may refer to it, we have not that in hand
just now. That is in the Report of the Committee on
the Confession of Faith, and it is proposed that that
should go down to presbyteries for suggestions."

The upshot was that in 1894 an Act was passed in the following
terms:

"Whereas the Declaratory Act, 1892, was passed to
remove difficulties and scruples which have been felt
by some in reference to the Declaration of Belief
required from persons who receive licence or are
admitted to office in this Church, the Assembly
hereby declare that the statements of doctrine
contained in the said Act are not thereby imposed
upon any of the Church's office-bearers as part of the
Standards of the Church; but that those who are
licensed or ordained to office in this Church, in
answering the Questions and subscribing the
Formula, are entitled to do so in view of the said
Declaratory Act."

The docking procedure with the United Presbyterian Church was
to be facilitated by use of precisely the same phraseology as they
themselves had used. The Formula of the United Presbyterian
Church had said, "in view of the explanations made in the
Declaratory Act." The Free Church Formula said more tersely,
"in view of the Declaratory Act."

The two Churches were fairly on course for marriage in the relatively near future. Both had passed Declaratory Acts modifying subscription to the Confession of Faith. Both required adherence only to "the substance of the faith." Both brought their respective acts into operation by allowing subscription "in view of the Declaratory Act."

For the Free Church, there remained the old problem that had soured relations in the 1863-73 debate, the question of Church establishment. In one of the clauses of the Declaratory Act, which spoke of "disclaiming intolerant or persecuting principles", and not committing office-bearers to any "principles inconsistent with liberty of conscience and the right of private judgement", the Constitutionalists saw an attempt by the majority to introduce disestablishment.

> "All reference to the duties of nations and their rulers
> to true religion and the Church of Christ is wholly
> omitted" they complain in their reasons of dissent,
> ..."while allusions to this teaching of the Confession
> is so introduced, as to imply that the doctrine is
> intolerant and persecuting; and thus, both directly and
> by implication, this distinctive doctrine of the Free
> Church is set aside."

Unlike the United Presbyterian Church, all whose office-bearers agreed with their Declaratory Act, the Constitutional Party, small enough in numbers, but still inveterately opposed to the changes that had been brought in, remained a sore in the side of the majority in the Free Church. If a united church was to enter into the union, they would have to be brought on board. If not, they would be bound to make trouble.

PART 4: JUBILEE WITHOUT CHEER

CHAPTER 2

MR MACFARLANE OF KILMALLIE AND RAASAY

Mr Macfarlane belonged to North Uist. Licensed in 1873, he had been close on twenty years a minister when the Declaratory Act appeared on the horizon. Three characteristics in particular marked him, his candidness, his modesty and his conviction. How many ministers will admit to being tempted to atheism. Yet Mr Macfarlane acknowledged that for the first three years of his ministry, and for a number of years thereafter, though to a decreasing extent, atheistic thoughts plagued him. Modesty made him shun the limelight. When a probationer in Dunoon, Dr Kennedy sent for him while visiting the town. Mr Macfarlane was shy even to appear in the presence of this man. Yet the kinship of spirit made shyness evaporate. Of Mr Macfarlane, Dr Kennedy said, "Do you know that I feel quite ashamed of myself while listening to his prayers at family worship in his own house," - a beautiful example of each esteeming other better than themselves. For all his modesty, Mr Macfarlane was a man of principle. The combination of these two - modesty and conviction - caused the prophet Jeremiah torture, ("Then I said, I will not make mention of him,...but his words were in mine heart as a burning fire shut up in my bones, and I was weary with forbearing, and I could not stay.") It must have affected Mr

Macfarlane in the same way. It also meant that for long periods
he might remain obscurely in the background till forced by
conviction to stand out.   .

For Mr Macfarlane, unlike Rev. Murdo MacAskill, the leader of
the Constitutional Party, the rough and tumble of ecclesiastical
debate with accusation and counter accusation was not his
milieu. The June convention of the Constitutional Party adopted
a Statement and Protest advising presbyteries and Sessions to
enter both documents into their books. Mr Macfarlane was there.
His role was   minor but suggestive.   He pronounced the
benediction. Prayer was more his element than the cut and thrust
of debate.

The meeting from which he sent out the protest to the 1892
Assembly was an illustration of his readiness, nevertheless, to
take a leading role in a time of crisis. He had been minister of
Kilmallie for only two years when the Declaratory Act was sent
down to the presbyteries as an overture in 1891. In the Spring,
he called a meeting of office-bearers from Oban to Kilmallie. "At
this meeting," says Rev. Donald Beaton, his biographer, "Mr
Macfarlane spoke calmly but deliberately of the far-reaching
effect of the changes contemplated and of the necessity of
adhering to the Bible and the Confession of Faith." The
following is the text of the petition and protest sent by Mr
Macfarlane to the Assembly of 1892.

> 1. "This meeting recalls with gratitude to Almighty
> God the fruit of the labours of the Westminster
> Assembly of Divines, embodied in their Confession of
> Faith and Larger and Shorter Catechisms, as well as
> the many blessings enjoyed by the Free Church whilst
> loyal to the Scriptural truths taught in these
> documents; asserts the continued adherence of those
> here present to the great scriptural doctrines of the

Confession of Faith, and its sufficiency to be, as heretofore, the chief Subordinate Standard of Doctrine in the Free Church.

II. "This meeting therefore deplores the changes of the doctrines of the Confession proposed in the Free Church Declaratory Act,

a. Because no Scriptural ground has been shown for the change now proposed;

b. Because the Act where not expressly opposed to the scriptural teaching of the Confession, is so indefinite and ambiguous in its language, that it will cover opinions subversive of that teaching;

c. Because the last clause of the proposed Act places a dangerous power in the hands of the General Assembly, and opens a door whereby fatal error may come to be openly tolerated and taught in the Church.

This meeting further emphatically protests against the conduct of men who have sworn to maintain, teach and defend our Confessional doctrines as the only terms upon which the Church would admit them into its offices, and demands of such to keep to their vows or, as honest men, to leave the Church.

And he respectfully requests that the Assembly should take into their serious consideration the foregoing Resolutions.

And your petitioner will ever pray.

D. Mcfarlane, Chairman."

From the mention in the first section of "the great Scriptural doctrines of the Confession", it is clear that it is not because of a hide-bound attachment to the Confession that Mr Macfarlane is opposing change, but because the Confession is based on Scripture. The first Act adopting the Confession of Faith in 1647 judged it to be "most orthodox, and grounded upon the word of God ." Doubtless, because of a tendency to find in it a kind of ready reference which would save one from the labour of searching Scripture at first hand, the Confession in theological debate could don the mantle of a primary rather than a secondary source of truth. Mr Macfarlane in any statements he makes on the matter is always careful to give first place to Scripture. By implication, he would not oppose change if "a scriptural ground" had been shown for the change.

Likewise, it is not merely that the Act is un-Scriptural. Section c. above speaks of "a dangerous power" placed in the hands of the General Assembly as a result of the likely passing of the Declaratory Act which "opens a door whereby fatal error may come to be openly tolerated and taught in the Church." Those who adopt the Act must have a blind faith in the orthodoxy of succeeding Assemblies to interpret the Confession of Faith in a Scriptural way. The very reason for the adoption of a Confession of Faith is that Assemblies may be kept in check when they would stray from the teaching of Scripture. The Confession of Faith, itself, by listing the number of canonical books and stating the authority to be accorded to them makes sure that Scripture will have final authority. No such check will now be in place. The Act is not only un-Scriptural, it is a-Scriptural, i.e. it holds the possibility of dispensing with Scripture altogether as the supreme rule of faith and life. The testimony of the Confession to the authority of Scripture, itself, may find itself outside "the substance of the Reformed faith" in the view of some future Assembly. When some professors like Henry Drummond were already saying that the statement of the Confession that the Scriptures had been authored by God was a relic of a by-gone age it was evident that Confessional shackles were not sufficient to keep order even before a Declaratory Act had been passed.

The opposition to the Act being on the basis of faith in the word of God, the line which that opposition may now take is made clear by the section in the Confession of Faith which says that a man's conscience is left free in matters of faith and worship from anything contrary to God's word or beside it. There is a striking likeness to the position of the Church of Scotland between 1839 and 1843. The Church of Scotland objected to the Government's invasion of the sphere of spiritual rule. The Constitutional party object to the invasion of an even more fundamental sphere. The sphere of ecclesiastical rule stems from the Scriptures. It is derivative. Fundamental to all such rights is the right to take Scripture as one's guide which all members of the mystical church can claim. The threat of the invasion of the sphere of ecclesiastical rule led the Church of Scotland not only to dissent from the law which made this invasion, (The Patronage Act), but to dissent followed by disobedience. The Constitutional Party must do the same in relation to the Declaratory Act. They would be implicated in its administration both at Session and Presbytery level when candidates come before the church courts for ordination. These candidates will be taking their vows "in view of the Declaratory Act". Hence, it is no wonder though we find the leader of the Constitutional Party, Mr MacAskill, say at the 1892 Assembly, (Assembly Proceedings, p. 162),

> "Even in the next two years before it became law, he had his rights and he should assert them. He had a right if anyone came before him for licence or ordination to put the question, 'Under which king, sir, do you want to live - under the Declaratory Act or the Confession of Faith in its old form?' And if anyone

said to him, 'I mean to take the Confession of Faith with the relief given by the Declaratory Act,' then he would refuse to licence him. He would refuse to ordain him. He should take all the consequences. He should refuse the licence, and he should refuse to ordain, and he should come up to that House, and he should see whether the Free Church of Scotland could depose him for contumacy."

On what was such refusal to submit based? Mr MacAskill makes clear in a letter to "The Scotsman" in August, 1893. In the 1892 Assembly, not only were reasons of dissent entered, but two protests were entered also which declared that the protesters would not have the Declaratory Act binding on them. A Mr Robertson of Rayne, who had been a follower of the Constitutional Party till 1892 wrote "The Scotsman" saying that the protest was not worth the paper it was written on.

Mr MacAskill replies as follows:

"The Free Church is just as spiritually free as her constitution allows and no more. As long as she acts within the limits of that constitution she is free to act as she pleases however unwise her action may sometimes be. But she is not spiritually free so as to act as either to violate or undermine that constitution. The moment she does so, opposition to her proceedings is not only lawful, but becomes the most solemn duty of all those who adhere to her constitution. And it is because we consider our Church through the action of an unfaithful majority in our General Assembly to have gone beyond the limits of her constitution that we have opposed - and mean to oppose and resist her action to the utmost. It is not spiritual liberty that is claimed in such proceedings by the majority, but licence for themselves to do as they please, and tyranny towards all who dare to oppose their unconstitutional actions. And I am surprised that one who has allowed all this (Mr Robertson) should write as he has done. His exposition in your columns of spiritual liberty, or rather the rights of the majority in the Church, however unconstitutional their action, and of the relative rights of General Assemblies and Presbyteries, savours more of spiritual slavery than of liberty and of the ultramontanism of Rome than of the spiritual liberty claimed by and enshrined in the fundamental documents of the Free Church. To that scriptural constitution, with its sacred legacy of spiritual rights and liberties the Constitutional party will strictly adhere, disregarding alike the sneers of tyranny of their opponents, and the defection of some of their weak-kneed friends."

In these developments, it is not surprising there should be a striking resemblance to elements we found in Luther's separation from the Church of Rome. Both the Constitutional Party and Luther were working from the same base - the veracity of Scripture. The fact that Luther was protesting against additions to the Scripture and the constitutionalists against subtractions makes no difference to the base from which both operate.

1. When Mr Macfarlane asserts that he will not accept the changes brought in by the Declaratory Act, certainly not till Scriptural foundations are given for the changes the Act will make, he is asserting **the right of private judgment** in opposition to absolute and blind obedience.

2. When Mr MacAskill and others presented their protest at the Assembly, they asserted the right of **liberty of conscience** within

the Church to oppose what they consider to be against Scripture. Here is the call of "semper reformanda" a call which may be brought into operation either when the Church departs from acknowledged truth as in this case, or when a person or group within the Church awakes to a truth hitherto neglected. As members of the mystical body of Christ, they have a right to call on the ministerial authorities of the Free Church to acknowledge the validity of their case. This determination to oppose was hardened into a firm plan of action when it was decided at the Constitutional Conference in June, 1892, to seek the entry of the protest in the books of lower courts such as presbyteries and sessions. This would give a firm basis for the kind of action contemplated by Mr McAskill, i.e. the refusal to allow men to take their vows under the Act.

3. There is the **refusal to submit to a call to blind obedience.** his is seen on two fronts.
a. There were many who sought to reassure the Constitutionalists that there was no real change to the stance of the Church. Dr Walter Ross Taylor, whose father had been a well known Highland clergyman in Thurso, and who, in contrast to his father's stance, had become one of the more prominent leaders of the more liberal section of the Church - he had proposed Dr Dodds as professor even after he had made clear his departure from stricter views of Biblical inspiration - said,

> "He was very sorry that their excellent friends would not take in the idea, which certainly was the true idea, that they had not proposed a substitute for the Confession, and had not proposed an addition to the Confession. They had simply, as honest men, declared what in their view was the interpretation of certain parts of the Confession."

Mr Macfarlane's petition to the 1892 Assembly, quoted above, will give a clear indication of how the Constitutionalists did not give mute acceptance to such assurances. Like the Bereans, they will judge for themselves whether what they are called upon to believe is according to Scripture or not.

b. If there was no hope that the Constitutional Party would agree that the Declaratory Act left their stance unchanged, attempts were made to assure them that a niche would be provided for them once the Act was passed in which they might find refuge. In 1892, Dr Rainy said,

> "Now I am very far from disregarding the dissent that has been expressed on this subject; and if this Act were an Act proposing to lay fresh obligations, specific obligations, on the minds of our office-bearers - either within the Church or about to enter it - if it were to lay some new Confessional burden on them, I should regard the dissent of much less than 23 Presbyteries as a very strong reason for halting and considering where we stand. But this Act will never be used in this way."

Dr Rainy seems to be speaking here rather of the way the Act will be used than of its content. The Constitutionalists, on their side, do not submit in implicit faith in such fulsome assurances. The whole protesting procedure shows how effectively they have learned the lesson of the spider and the fly. Once one goes across a certain boundary, return may well be impossible. In that case it is much safer to remain frankly separate.

4. If it is asked by what authority one can do all this and still remain within the Free Church, there is an underlying emphasis on **the headship of Christ,** and the corresponding **priesthood of all believers** in the letter to "The Scotsman" above. Mr MacAskill speaks of the rights claimed by Mr Robertson for the majority in the higher courts of the Free Church as savouring "more of spiritual slavery than of liberty and of the ultramontanism of Rome than of the spiritual liberty claimed by and enshrined in the fundamental documents of the Free

Church." Ultramontanism was the doctrine that the Pope had absolute authority. Mr MacAskill denies that the majority in the Free Church have such authority. "There is no such head of the Church on earth - no power either civil or ecclesiastical, that can interfere between my conscience and the mind of Christ as I see it in His Word." (H.W. Montcrieff, "The Free Church Principle"). It is because the Constitutional Party do not hear the voice of Christ in the Declaratory Act that they claim the right to oppose the Act. The fact that those they oppose are the majority in the Church courts, and therefore are able to carry the day when it comes to the vote is neither here nor there. As mentioned in chapter 2 it is a sovereign right given by Christ that the Church be ruled by Scripture. It is impossible to know whether the Church will be led by Scripture or not, both because of indefiniteness of wording, because no Scriptural proofs are given, and because of the possibility of undermining the Scriptural teaching of the Confession by unscrupulous use of the phrase, "the substance of the reformed faith", the right of examination of such legislation according to Scripture is denied. The imposition of such legislation is tyranny. Refusal to submit is a duty according to the liberty granted in the Confession of Faith.

5. The ultimate upshot is that there is a divided Church. It could not be otherwise. Later in the same speech in the 1892 General Assembly, Mr MacAskill speaks of the effect the passing of the Declaratory Act will have;

> "The moment they got this Act passed, they had two classes of ministers in the Church - one that took their Standards without any relief, and the other that took them with the relief the Act was designed to afford. In this way they would have two classes of ministers, two classes of elders, two classes of deacons, and two Confessions of faith in the one Church."

There is, of course, a difference from the lack of uniformity where two sections in the one Church agree to differ. Those who take relief under the Declaratory Act are taking relief from an Act that has been passed as a binding law and constitution. They will expect that all will conform to the Act. Those who do not will argue from the same premise that the Act must be suspended. They claim a just right to be ruled according to Scripture. This Act is so indefinite that it is impossible even to make that judgment when the Act has been passed as a binding law. If they may claim that it is suspended for one, it is suspended for all. (This rule applies in civil law, too. If the Maastricht Treaty had been rejected by one nation, e.g. Denmark, then it would have lost its application to any. The whole legislative process would have had to begin from the outset). What unites the two sides, as I hope to show in the next chapter, is the court of heaven. As long as the appeal of the Constitutional Party remains before that court, and the majorty do not reject the appeal, the two sides may remain in a kind of unity in division.

In one of his more revealing moments, Dr Rainy tells in the 1892 debate of what the effect of the Declaratory Act will be. He assures the Assembly that the Assembly will retain its power of guarding against any abuse of the liberty granted by the Act, but it is clear that the Church will be on an entirely new footing.

> "And how will that be guarded against? It will be guarded against by the Church retaining the same power of judging the just sense of this Declaratory Act as it has to expound the just sense of the Confession of Faith - (applause) - that is to say, the Church will judge what is within this limit, what is consistent and not consistent with the substance of the Reformed faith."

The issue could not have been put more starkly. What the Confession of Faith was yesterday as the doctrinal basis of the

Church, the substance of the Reformed faith is today. It is this the minority protest against.

The Free Church, according to Dr Rainy's vision, will become a broad church containing elements that stretch from the most die-hard conservatives who feel that the sun rises and sets on the Westminster Assembly of divines, to those who push the phrase, "the substance of the Reformed faith" to its limits and beyond. In Dr Rainy's view, however, there will be unity in this diversity. All will subscribe to "the substance of the Reformed faith." The only difference is that for the conservatives, that substance expands to fill the whole Confession. For the more liberal wing, the substance contracts to that fraction of the whole which will be determined by any particular Assembly to represent fundamental truth.

The Constitutionalists spurn this unity. To them the Confession is not performing its true function if it is not binding upon all. The determination of Mr MacAskill, under his protest, to refuse to allow any in his own presbytery at least, to take refuge under the Act is an evidence that he considered the Act suspended. Only thus could he have any leverage in refusing to grant the relief in the Act to those who sought it.

As a result, the lack of uniformity between the opposing parties as seen by Dr Rainy and by Mr MacAskill are quite diverse. For Dr Rainy the diversity consists in a variety of personal belief. For Mr MacAskill, the lack of uniformity lies in a fundamental division in outlook as to what the Free Church stands for. The doctrinal constitution is the Confession of Faith. Any lessening of that authority and the Free Church ceases to be the Free Church. The diverse elements in Dr Rainy's view of the Church may be bed-fellows in the one Church. By contrast, the two sections in Mr MacAskill's ultimately cannot. Opposing elements, one of which claims the Confession of Faith should be binding on all and the other which advocates an indefinite relaxation in subscription to the doctrines of the Confession cannot be reconciled. The only way out of the impasse is that one or the other capitulate.

The protest of the Constitutional Party, then, contains a complex of ideas. It is an expression of private judgement. It claims Confessional liberty of conscience within the Church. As part of that liberty it claims personal freedom from the provisions of the Declaratory Act. The right of personal freedom stems from the right of private judgement, and the right to refuse to submit to implicit faith. They cannot submit to what is contrary to Scripture. The only way the assurances of the majority that they would not be compromised in accepting the provisions of the Declaratory Act can have any credibility involves uncertainties over which they have no control. They make appeal for the exercise of all these rights to the authority of the head of the church, Jesus Christ, who rules His church by the laws of Scripture which the Declaratory Act spurns.

It may be objected that of the five elements illustrated in the stance of the Constitutional Party in the protest of 1892, (pp. 104-107), only one (the right of private judgement, p. 104) owes its origin directly to a document written by Mr Macfarlane. The others are deduced from the August letter of Mr MacAskill to "The Scotsman". Can we be certain that Mr Macfarlane subscribed to these views? In the next chapter I will go on to show there is abundance of evidence to show that Mr Macfarlane fully shared these views of Mr MacAskill.

PART 4: JUBILEE WITHOUT CHEER

CHAPTER 3

MR MACFARLANE, THE PROTESTER, 1892

Perhaps the clearest expression given by Mr Macfarlane of what went on between 1892 and 1893 occurs in his "Memoir and Remains" edited by Rev. D. Beaton. It was written after 1900, (since he speaks of the 20th century in the course of his address), and in all likelihood in 1905 or 1916, (since at the end of the piece he mentions a movement for union between the Free Church and the Free Presbyterian. In both these years there were proposals for union). The date is relatively immaterial. The account given in "Memoir and Remains of Rev. D. MacDonald, Sheildaig" is much more sketchy and does not touch on the vital question of how Mr Macfarlane regarded the protests entered in 1892 and 1893.

The account is the substance of a lecture delivered at Kishorn which takes the form of an imaginary trial between two parties, D.A., a young, self-conceited stripling, who represents the Declaratory Act, and C.F., who clearly personifies the party which had supported the Confession of Faith, "an old party of long experience, of mature judgement, and highly respected by experienced and well-grounded followers in the doctrines and practices of the faith as clearly set forth in the Word of God." There is almost a playfulness in the presentation of his ponderous subject in this dramatic form which would not have passed unappreciated by his rustic audience.

By way of introduction, Mr Macfarlane says that the case of contention between the two had been repeatedly tried in the Courts of the Church. At length it was decided in favour of the younger man, (D.A.). This brings us without more ado to the 1892 Assembly when the Declaratory Act was passed.

"The young party had many followers in a back-sliding age, but the old party protested and appealed to a higher court - the Court of heaven - to finally decide the case; as there was no higher court to appeal to."

The above quotation shows two things. First, it shows that Mr Macfarlane, though not present in the Assembly in the 1892, did not confine himself to a protest prior to the Assembly, but knew of and associated himself with the protest entered *after* the Declaratory Act had been passed.

Second, it shows the interpretation which Mr Macfarlane put on the protest. It was not an act of separation, even though the minority had been defeated; it was the fruit in the General Assembly of an appeal to the Court of heaven. As argued in the previous chapter, the acceptance of such a protest would suspend the passage of the Act concerned.

"God was the Judge, speaking through His Word, and it was the standard by which the case was tried and finally settled. The court-house was filled with anxious listeners, among whom were many ministers and office-bearers, who were self-confident that the case would be settled in favour of D.A., as it had been in the lower courts. But the case was not to be settled or decided this time by majorities, but by the Judge who is just in all his ways and holy in all his works. He would decide the case impartially in favour of the one who had the truth on his side."

This paragraph gives further illumination. It shows what may be inferred from the fact that the protest was received by the Supreme Court. It meant that both sides admitted the right of deferring to the court of heaven. Had it been only those who appealed and protested who awaited the judgement of the court of heaven, this would have indicated that the protest had been refused, and the protesters would have been forced in a short time to leave. Both sides accept the appeal to the highest court where decisions are not come to by majorities. Hence for the time being, the protesters are tolerated within the Church. If there is any doubt about this, it is resolved on p.162 where Mr Macfarlane says that a primary part of the 1893 protest - a year later - was "the arrogant manner in which D.A. tried to compel all to accept his views." Prior to that period, by inference, they were not compelled.

When did this trial take place? It took place directly after the protest had been tabled. Those who, in conventions or church courts, took issue with the Act and refused to implement it reflect in their stance the decision of heaven. Mr Macfarlane is revealed as adhering to three of the points touched on in the last chapter besides the one already discussed, viz. private judgement.

a. He believes in liberty of conscience. The Declaratory Act had already been passed by large majorities. Yet there is no mention of separation. This is because Christian liberty means serving God out of a true heart and willing mind. Such liberty should be acknowledged by Church courts, giving those who conscientiously disagree on Scriptural grounds the right to protest. Montcrieff's "The Practice of the Free Church of Scotland" says, (p.93),

> "The Free Church maintains most emphatically that
> no authority in the hands of fallible men, such as the
> authority of the General Assembly, has any absolute

rule over the consciences of believers, and that every
one of her members may appeal to the Great Head of
the Church against any such merely ministerial
authority." (This statement is taken over into the
Manual of Practice of the Free Presbyterian Church
with the substitution of "Synod" for "General
Assembly").

As noted above, the majority in 1892 accepted this appeal by the
reception of the protest.

b. He does not believe in the call to follow a blind faith. That the
Declaratory Act called for this has already been pointed out in
previous chapters.

c. The third point illustrated in the lecture is the headship of
Christ over the Church, not as a mere nominal headship, but as a
headship which must be viewed as an active element in the day-
to-day rule of the Church. Without doubt the Headship
contemplated by Mr Macfarlane is no mere nominal headship
like that of the Moderates but an active Headship which as surely
as in Acts of the Apostles, hands down judgement on the issues
debated by earthly courts, and influences their proceedings. The
old party protest and appeal to this higher court "to finally decide
the issue." Making it doubly sure that it is clear that no earthly
court influences the outcome, Mr Macfarlane says, "But the case
was not to be settled or decided this time by majorities, but by the
Judge who is just in all his ways and holy in all His works. He
would decide the case impartially in favour of the one who had
truth on his side."

It is the protesters who have appealed. It is the protesters who
await the judgement. It is they who will be bound by the result.
Judgement is finally given.

"I approve of every statement in C.F.'s document, as
all statements therein are supported by my Word of

truth, and I, as Judge of all, through my word, condemn D.A. and acquit C.F. from the charge brought against him by his accuser."

Is it any wonder, then, that through the period, 1892-93, Mr Macfarlane felt justified in opposing the Declaratory Act outright. One illustration of the determination to abide by the protest of 1892, and the importance of that protest in maintaining their witness, is seen in an answer to one particular Reason of Dissent ("Such a Protest is useless to accomplish any practical purpose, and the only effective remedy by any court of the Church disapproving of an Act of Assembly is to overture the General Assembly to amend or repeal the Act disapproved of"), entered when the Protest was inscribed in the books of the Presbytery of Abertarff.

The answer is as follows:

"The Presbytery look upon this Protest for the purpose of resisting the Declaratory Act far more hopeful and useful than overturing the Assembly for its repeal; for no-one believes the Assembly shall do so, while the Protest secures us against compliance with the said Act, and is a bond of union among those who mean to resist it."

Why is it more hopeful? It is the Assembly itself which has allowed the protest and appeal to go ahead. As long as the protesters are able to abide by their protest, the Declaratory Act cannot truly be brought into action. Indeed, the following is a quotation which shows that this view was Dr Rainy's own judgement on the suspending power of a protest. In speaking of the entry of another protest in the Skye Presbytery he says in 1893 as follows,

> "The Declaratory Act was an Act of relief, and, of course, in many respects it was right for the brethren concerned to continue to conduct their duties upon the old view which they had always had on these doctrines which ought to guide them. But to protest against this Act was a protest that denied it all force and validity in any sense whatever. It was a claim to suspend the operation of the Act in all respects. It sought to avoid the effect it was intended to have, namely, that of relief."

The Declaratory Act was meant to change the contract of association. As long as some refused to admit this change, the Act remained ineffective, since the Act must have an equal effect across the whole church. If only the protesters would drop their protest, and allow relief to be given, they could take their stance in this new Church preaching as faithfully as ever the old doctrines, just so long as they would admit the right of others to avail themselves of the relief. It is this state of affairs the protesters refuse to admit, and which their bond of union aims to prevent.

In passing, it is worth noting that the above Answer to Reasons of Dissent shows how the account in Rev. D. MacDonald's biography needs to be supplemented. In this account Mr Macfarlane says,

> "The separation took place in the year, 1893. If it be asked, Why did it not take place in 1892 when the change was made? the answer is, some did speak of separating at that time, but there was a cry among the Constitutionalists to keep together to act in concert,

and to wait till they should exhaust all constitutional means in their power to persuade the Assembly to reconsider their action with a view to their rescinding of the Declaratory Act. At the Assembly of 1893, there was an effort made by the Constitutionalists to this effect; but the Assembly refused to rescind the Act.....There was, therefore, no alternative left for us but to separate."

This, of course, is wholly true, but it is not the whole truth. Where "The Declaratory Act in Court" together with the above answer to the reason of dissent supplements this account is in showing that "the keeping together to act in concert" was a keeping together under protest, and that what gave particular power to the effort to have the Declaratory Act rescinded in 1893 was that the Constitutional Party had been under protest between 1892 and 1893. The Church had allowed this protest. Therefore, the Constitutionalists could claim that the Act was not binding.

d. As it is, the protesters claimed the right of protest and claimed that they blocked the final passage of the Act. This may well be why Mr Macfarlane says in his protest at the Session in Kilmallie, that the Church had taken only

> "*a decided step in the direction of* imperilling the interests of Divine truth, and of innovation upon the doctrinal and ecclesiastical constitution of the Free Church."

In Mr Macfarlane's description of the trial of D.A. by the Court of heaven, D.A., significantly, is not expelled immediately. The Judge says,

> "As I am a long-suffering God, and delight in mercy, while judgement is my strange work, I will give D.A.'s followers an opportunity of renouncing their

errors, and of returning to sound doctrine, but if not, their blood shall be upon their own head."

"The opportunity of renouncing their errors" stemmed from the continued existence of a protesting minority still in integral relationship with the Church in the conduct of its affairs. This led on to a motion in the 1893 Assembly by Dr Winter that the overtures and petitions for rescinding the Declaratory Act be referred to a committee which would report to next General Assembly. The refusal of that petition together with the "freezing out" of the protesting minority meant the final end of the protesting witness.

It will be seen from the above that Mr Macfarlane acknowledged in the course of his separation in 1892-93 all the key elements that we have already drawn from the rights granted by the Confession of Faith.

In the next chapter I will go on to show that the primary reason for separation in 1893 was not the passage of the Declaratory Act *per se*, but the fact it was impossible any longer to exercise liberty of conscience within the Free Church, and impossible to remove one's neck from the yoke of an absolute and blind obedience.

PART 4: JUBILEE WITHOUT CHEER

CHAPTER 4

MR MACFARLANE, THE PROTESTER, 1893

In the preceding chapter, I considered the implications of the earlier part of the lecture, "The Declaratory Act in Court". This earlier part refers to the actions of the 1892 Assembly. The latter part deals with the 1893 Assembly, and the response of Mr Macfarlane to the refusal of the rights of protest in this Assembly.

Directly after the statement that the Judge would give an opportunity of renouncing their errors to D.A. and his followers, the Judge addresses D.A. asking him what he was to do.

> "D.A. refused to retract any of his statements, holding that, according to his opinion, he did not forsake the truth. The Judge - do you think yourself wiser than I?"

This passage clearly refers to the 1893 refusal even to consider revising the Declaratory Act.

> "There was great commotion over the decision of the Judge. Those who adhered to C.F. protested against the arrogant manner in which D.A. tried to compel all to accept his views, and by their protest and

determined adherence to C.F., made a faithful stand according to the grace given to them for the original standards of faith and practice held by the fathers in 1843, their eyes looking unto the hills from whence cometh their help."

When compared with the text of the protest of Mr Macfarlane in 1893, it is evident he is here giving the essential parts of that document. There are three elements,

1. "The determined adherence to C.F.."

> 1. "I, the undersigned minister of the Free Church, in my own name and in the name of all who may adhere to me, declare that, whatever I may subsequently do, neither my conscience nor my ordination vows allow me to act under what has now been made law in this Church." (This "determined adherence to C.F." is essentially a repetition of the protest of 1892).

2. The protest "against the arrogant manner in which D.A. tried to compel all to accept his views."

> 2. "I also protest against the despotic power exercised by a majority of the office-bearers of this Church in making changes in her creed and constitution, which are *ultra vires* of any majority in the face of any protesting minority."

3. The statement that they are making a faithful stand for "the original standards of faith and practice held by the fathers of 1843."

> "I declare that I claim my sacred and civil rights according to the terms of contract agreed upon

> between me and the Free Church at my ordination,
> and in accordance with the creed and constitution of
> the Free Church in the year 1843."

Mr Macfarlane's protest in 1893 goes beyond the statement in no. 2 and gives a means of interpreting it. It is not clear why the Assembly in 1893 were "arrogant" in compelling all to accept her views. It is usually accepted that if a majority gain the decision it is only justice that they demand that the minority submit. This can hardly be construed as arrogance. This statement is only meaningful if supplemented by the Protest, itself. The "arrogant manner" answers to "the despotic power exercised by a majority of the office-bearers of this Church in making changes....which are ultra vires of any majority *in the face of any protesting minority."* This is a protest both for the rights of protest which the minority have exercised as a specific means of preserving their rights, and against the over-riding of these rights. It is not simply as a minority that the Constitutionalists have resisted submission to the Declaratory Act, but specifically as a protesting minority. This reflects the "Answers to Reasons of Dissent" at the Abertarff Presbytery, where it is stated that the Protest secures the minority "against compliance with the said Act."

(Note that the right of protest due to referral of the case to the court of heaven is inferred, since not till the Assembly in 1893 does Mr Macfarlane speak of "despotic power". By implication, between 1892 and 1893 they were free from such coercion).

How compulsion was brought to bear on the protesting minority is easy to trace from the course of the proceedings in the 1893 Assembly.

1. The presbytery protests which the Constitutional Party had entered wherever possible after the June 1892 Convention were ruled out of order by the 1893 Assembly. That these were considered vital for the witness of the party may be seen by

another of the Answers to Reasons of Dissent in the Abertarff Presbytery:

> ".....This Presbytery, entertaining no such scruples regarding any of the doctrines of the Confession, are at liberty to reject and protest against said Act, for they cannot conceive how, as individuals, they are at liberty to reject it, but that the Presbytery is bound to submit to it."

The Presbytery Protests came before the Assembly on May 20th. Principal Rainy's motion was as follows,

> "The Assembly order the deletion of the protests and declarations referred to from the Records of the Presbyteries of Skye and Lochcarron, but not having the document in the case of Abertarff before them, they pass from consideration of it."

The technicality that the protest in the books of the Presbytery of Abertarff was not expunged must have afforded Mr Macfarlane little comfort. He was by that time, at any rate, in the Presbytery of Skye. Since the protest in that Presbytery was deleted, the Presbytery would, according to the view of the protesters in the Abertarff Presbytery, of which Mr Macfarlane had been one of the leading spokesmen, be bound to submit to the Act.

This, then, the deletion of the Presbytery protests, is one of the reasons why Mr Macfarlane protested against the despotic power in "trying to compel all to accept their views."

2. Even though the Presbytery protests had gone, the protest entered at the last General Assembly after the Declaratory Act had been passed still stood.

This leads us to one of the most curious characteristics of the 1893 Assembly, viz., the attitude of Dr Rainy to the question of protest.

a. He denies the possibility of a protest at the Assembly after an Act has been passed.

The following are Dr Rainy's views, (p. 62).

> "A protest really meant a denial in the meantime, a denial of the validity of the action that was protested against, that it is null and void in an inferior court. They protested and appealed, they protested and complained, and their protest suspended the operation of the Act that had been passed until it was renewed. *That was why there was no such thing as a protest against the decision of the General Assembly.*"

It will be seen directly how different the view of Dr Rainy was from that of Mr Macfarlane. For Dr Rainy, the highest court is the General Assembly. For Mr Macfarlane, it is the court of heaven. For Dr Rainy, protest is meaningless at the General Assembly since there is no higher court to appeal to. For Mr Macfarlane, it is instinct with meaning since it flows from appeal to the highest court of all, i.e. the court of heaven.

b. Dr Rainy makes no mention of the protests that had, in fact, been entered at the 1892 Assembly. If he was so concerned that *Presbytery* protests be deleted, must not these *Assembly* Protests be attended to with even greater urgency? Instead, he goes on to say that the right to protest had never been admitted, "because a protest was a claim to suspend the action of the things protested against." Dr Rainy must very well have known about the existence of the 1892 protests. If these protests are there on the books of the Assembly, and they still are, why does he not admit the consequence that these protests suspend the operation of the Act that has been passed, (i.e. the Declaratory Act), until it, (the Declaratory Act) was renewed. This is despotic power of the highest order. Just pretend that something objectionable does not exist and it will vanish away! Is it any wonder Mr Macfarlane protests against despotic power of this nature, when the main plank by which the Constitutional Party had kept its integrity 1892-93 was whipped from beneath their feet?

In this, at any rate, Mr Macfarlane agrees with Dr Rainy, that as long as a protesting minority are in the Church, acting upon their protest, the Act cannot be said to be binding. That is the full meaning of his statement that the changes are *ultra vires* in the face of a protesting minority. Conversely, take the protesting minority away, and nothing will stand in the way of the full implementation of the Act .

3. The questions and formula were so interpreted that both parties could claim the relief they sought. The party for change could say they were able to avail themselves of the Declaratory Act. The party opposing change were invited to use an interpretaton which seemed to assert no change had taken place. Quite apart from the dubious morality involved, the upshot could not satisfy the protesters. Their protest, they claimed, should suspend the Act. Where any party availed themselves of the act, the protest was nullified.

In the course of the debate about protests, Dr Rainy says the following,

> "The general principle was most important that the questions as they stood, and the formula as it stood, must be signed as they stood, each person on his own responsibility making up his mind as to what they meant, and the relation of his own convictions to that meaning. He meant to say there was no difficulty

raised for men by the questions and formula. The questions and formula said nothing about the Declaratory Act, and in no sense imposed it, and there was therefore no difficulty in that respect."

There are two irreconcilables that must be reconciled. Those who seek relief want relief immediately. They are told that it is possible to gain relief by taking their own meaning out of the Questions and Formula. The following is the way this particular rabbit was drawn out of the hat. (Comment has already been made on this point in 1/2.) First I will give the full quotation of the relevant question.

"Do you sincerely own and believe the whole doctrine contained in the Confession of Faith, approven by former General Assemblies of this Church, to be founded upon the Word of God; and do you acknowledge the same as the confession of your faith....."

Both Questions and Formula have the phrase, "approven by former General Assemblies of this Church" describing the length and breadth of the "whole doctrine of the Confession of Faith" which the subscriber professed to take as the confession of his faith. Immediately the General Assembly was over, the 1892 Assembly became a "former General Assembly of this Church". In this way, the subscriber could claim to subscribe to "the whole doctrine of the Confession approven by the 1892 General Assembly." (As already quoted from Dr Stalker in the Glasgow presbytery, there had been other Declaratory Acts which came into operation in the same way). This Assembly had passed the Declaratory Act. Since this Act required allegiance to no more than "the substance of the Reformed faith" this "substance of the reformed faith" contained in the Confession became the limits of "the whole doctrine", according to the broad party, which was all that bound any person who wished to avail himself of the relief given in the Act.

The other section seek relief from administering the Act, a relief that is impossible to gain if a meaning can be won from the Questions and Formula which allows others to take advantage of the Declaratory Act. They are told simply to take their own meaning out of the Questions and Formula, and content their consciences with the fact that the Questions and Formula do not mention the Declaratory Act. It is not difficult to see how they might take that meaning. If "whole doctrine" is taken as qualifying primarily "contained in the Confession of Faith", rather then "approven by General Assemblies", and this - the whole doctrine of the Confession - is the doctrine which is "approven by former General Assemblies of the Church", then no General Assembly can change the Confession of Faith. The utmost a Declaratory Act should do is declare the meaning of the Confession. It should not modify it. Hence, no person can avail himself of any view of the Declaratory Act which he may claim modifies the Confession of Faith.

One can imagine a situation which must have occurred many times over between 1892 and 1900. A candidate for the ministry comes forward who intends to avail himself of the freedom granted by the Declaratory Act. The presbytery in which he takes his vows is a presbytery in which there is a minister of the Constitutional Party. When the candidate says that he takes the whole doctrine of the Confession of Faith as the confession of his faith, he is saying inwardly, "as modified by the Declaratory Act." The Constitutional minister is saying, "You are binding yourself to the whole doctrine of the Confession of Faith. Hence, I am not at this time administering the Declaratory Act." The great difference between the two is that the Constitutional minister is not protected in the inference he makes, while the other is. Were the matter brought out into the open, and both were to declare the meanings they privately take from the ordination service, the Constitutional minister could not challenge the newly ordained minister. The Church protects him in taking his vows "in view of the Declaratory Act."

The Questions and Formula did not impose the Declaratory Act. It could be said they did something much worse. If used as Dr. Rainy indicates they appear to become accessories to the sin of perjury. The Confession of Faith says that "an oath is to be taken in the plain and common sense of the words, without equivocation or mental reservation." Dr Rainy says there is no "plain or common sense" meaning in the words of question and formula. Hence it is impossible to prevent equivocation and mental reservation. "I take these words" each signatory may say, "in this particular meaning which suits my convictions." Thus the Free Church may be made as conservative or liberal as each individual may wish to make it. The contract of association has gone by the board. Hence the continuing need of the protest to provide real opposition.

Later on in the Assembly, Dr Rainy said,

> "One of the most important things in the view of some of them, was making it quite distinct to their brethren that the Declaratory Act was not meant to impose fresh Confessional obligations upon anybody, and they put that in the preamble; but it did not appear to have met with a great deal of response in the quarters where they desired it to operate."

Is it any wonder? The preamble said "some" required relief. The Confession of Faith was meant to impose a united doctrinal stance on the whole Church. Where the Questions and Formula were used as above, they brought disunity into the very fabric of the Church's operations, and did so all the more ominously that the disunity was hidden by fair-sounding words.

For these obvious reasons, the denial of protests entered at Presbytery, the denial even of the existence of the protests entered at the previous General Assembly, and the forcing of the protesting minority into a dishonourable arrangement whereby the law is brought into operation by means of the advanced party taking advantage of ambiguity in the meaning of the questions and formula, Mr Macfarlane protests against the despotic power of the majority. This is not a protest against the Act itself. It is what it says it is, a protest against the denial of the rights of private judgement, against having to submit to implicit faith in the promise that they will not be subject to the Act, against the denial of liberty of conscience, against refusal to hear the voice of Christ speaking through the protesting minority, and against the sudden abolition of the protesting lobby when it had been allowed to continue its protest from 1892 to 1893.

Before leaving the subject, there is one further point to be considered. In the Memoir and Remains of Rev. D. MacDonald, Mr Macfarlane says,

> "In the year 1892, the General Assembly of the Free Church of Scotland passed a Declaratory Act, in terms of the Barrier Act, into a binding law of the Church whereby the Creed and constitution of the church were completely altered."

In 1893, in the Protest which he entered after the refusal of the Assembly to reconsider the Act, Mr Macfarlane begins his protest,

> "Whereas by the action of the General Assembly of 1892 in passing the Declaratory Act into a law of the Church, and by that Act being retained in her constitution, the Church in our opinion ceases to be the true representative of the Free Church of Scotland."

Does it not seem that the quotation from Mr MacDonald's book indicates that the Free Church ceased to be the true representative in 1892, while the protest says this happened in 1893?

In reality, this only gives further credence to the view that the Act, in Mr Macfarlane's view, was suspended. The acceptance of the protest in 1892 brought both parties before the court of heaven. Hence, though passed on earth, it remained to the court of heaven to give final verdict. Where that right of liberty of conscience was in exercise, the Declaratory Act was in a limbo between the two Assemblies. Only with the despotic ending of the right of liberty of conscience in denial of the exercise of protest did the Act become operative. Only then did the Free Church cease to be "the true representative of the Free Church of Scotland."

Mr Macfarlane, then, was totally consistent throughout. Because the protest of 1892 was accepted, he could stay in, since this acceptance raised the matter to a higher court. The two opposites could remain together in the one Church, pending the judgement of the higher court. The same principles that kept Mr Macfarlane in the Free Church in 1892, are those which drove him out in 1893. He strives for the rights of private judgement, liberty of conscience and the right to oppose efforts to impose absolute and blind obedience in 1892, and when these are granted, he stays in. In 1893 he seeks for the same rights and because these are denied he must leave, still appealing to God, "even to him who made heaven and earth, trusting that he would sustain them in providence as well as in grace."

PART 5: A ROOT OF BITTERNESS

CHAPTER 1

THE STUDENTS

There were others who joined Mr Macfarlane in 1893 when he made his separation. These were students who had an entirely different relationship to the Free Church than Mr Macfarlane had in the period 1892-93. The students separated from the Constitutional Party in June 1892. At a meeting on November 2, 1892, the students had a meeting of which the following was the outcome.

> "Seeing the Declaratory Act is now an integral part of the constitution of the Free Church of Scotland, we, the undersigned, have ceased to prosecute our studies with a view to the ministry of that Church, as now constituted."

Allan Mckenzie   Divinity
James S. Sinclair   "
Alex. McRae   "
Neil Cameron   "

Rod. Mckenzie   "
John Mcleod   "
George Mckay   Arts
Donald Beaton   "
Neil MacIntyre   "

The most of these names are deeply revered in the history of the Free Presbyterian Church. The beginning of the Church, however, can only be understood when it is recognised that the principles on which they made their separation from the Free Church as regards liberty of conscience were quite different from those of Mr Macfarlane.

It has already been said that the protest which Mr Macfarlane adhered to in 1892 involved for him the right of private judgement, the right to appeal to the Head of the Church, the right to resist implicit faith, the right to remain in the Free Church refusing to administer the Declaratory Act, at least until areas of uncertainty were cleared up. The students denied the right of protest, with these associated rights.

This began at the Constitutional Conference in June, 1892. In the Church History, p. 72, Mr Cameron (who was himself one of these students), says,

> "What had been done at the above meeting had not in the least degree relieved the consciences of the Constitutional Party or those adhering to them from the unscriptural teaching of the Declaratory Act and the heretical views which were now with the authority of the Church to be protected within its pale; and until the Constitutional ministers (Mr Macfarlane included) would take effective steps to relieve themselves and the people from these pernicious

doctrines, the students would not acknowledge the courts of the Free Church."

What had been done at the above meeting, as noted earlier, had been the decision to fight on under cover of a protest. Mr Macfarlane, it is needless to insist once again, considered the protest as an appeal to the great Head of the Church, an effective means of opposing the Declaratory Act. In seconding the entry of the protest at the Presbytery of Abertarff, he says he felt bound, not only by his ordination vows, but as a professing Christian, to use every legitimate means to oppose this Declaratory Act forced upon them by the General Assembly. To the students, this means was illegitimate.

The reason why the students opposed the legitimacy of the protest is set out by John McLeod in the February 22 edition of "The Northern Chronicle."

"Others again rely with equal confidence on the defence afforded them by the statement and protest adopted at the Convention in Inverness, June 14th, 1892. The refuge is a refuge of lies. The "Statement" tells us that the Declaratory Act is a decided step in the direction of innovating on the Doctrinal constitution of the Free Church. The Act is more. Were it no more than that, the policy of staying in might be justified. But there is good reason to fear that the description of the Act has been adapted to the intended policy of the minority, and not that the policy has been adapted to meet the real nature of the crisis. The "Statement" is insufficient; the protest is illegal; yet Highland presbyteries are busy tying themselves to each. Many have tied themselves who are unsatisfied with statement and protest alike, and so have tied their hands from all future action. Defiant protests against the law of the Church are plain breaches of ordination vows. At ordination, every office-bearer vows submission to the lawful courts of the Church. Refusing to acknowledge a law of the Church is not obedience, it is contumacy, if the church is on its old foundation. If the courts of the Church have a new constitution, are not vows broken by those who remain in integral and vital union with these courts. Every office-bearer at ordination vowed to assert, maintain and defend the constitution of the Church - with a changed constitution such a thing cannot be done in the Church. Protesting is contumacy. Remaining in is unfaithfulness to solemn vows. In each line of action ordination vows are trampled underfoot."

In ordinary circumstances, it would be an impertinence for me to comment on the positions of either Mr Macfarlane or the students, living so far away as I now do from the stir of battle in which both were engaged. The consequences have been so serious, however, of not showing the distinction in their relative stances over the year, 1892-93, that it must be done.

The students allege that Mr Macfarlane's refuge - a legitimate means of opposing the Act according to him - is a "refuge of lies." I have already devoted an chapter to reply to the arguments set out by Mr Macleod. Suffice it to say that such an analysis does not begin to do justice to the background of the heavenly court against which Mr Macfarlane sees his protest legitimately presented. It does not do justice to the 20th chapter of the Confession of Faith which along with all other sections the office-bearers take as the confession of their faith. It does not give due weight to the rights of the mystical church as over against the ministerial church and the duty of the ministerial church to take these rights into consideration. It does not begin to do justice to the fact that church courts have the obligation to rule consistently with the liberties of those under their rule, and if the office-bearers who make them up have obligations to consider the courts with due reverence, the courts equally have obligations to the office-bearers. It does not mention that the powers that God has ordained are not meant to snuff out liberty of conscience but to uphold and preserve it, as truly as the individuals in a church are to uphold and preserve the rights of the rulers.

In an independent church the students might have been able to form a denomination of their own in 1892. In a presbyterian church they could not. Ordination comes through a presbytery. A presbytery must have a minimum of two ministers in its make-up. The step of leaving the Free Church before any of its ministers left could have been fraught with the utmost danger if they thought that their calling was to continue working among the people with whom they felt the strongest spiritual bonds.

Even before the Declaratory Act had been passed, the students were acutely aware of their predicament. In a meeting in Oban, 13th April, 1892, Allan Mckenzie, one of the divinity students addressed the meeting thus:

"The Word of God is worth living for, it is worth dying for. (Enthusiastic applause.) He would like the men with the difficulties and scruples to come forward and state them; he had never met them. And now they asked the people of the Free Church, were the Students to be thrown out of the Free Church? For they would never, God giving them grace to resist, sign such a document as the Declaratory Act. (Great Applause.) Their consciences would not let them. As they had to stand before the bar of God's judgement, and as they hoped to see Christ, they could not go on to be ministers of the Free Church to proclaim the extraordinary doctrines of this Declaratory Act."

Though for the preceding year they had held opposing views on the power of the constitutional protest, in 1893, the students found refuge with Mr Macfarlane and Mr MacDonald. They were united in two most essential issues. They believed the Declaratory Act undermined the constitution of the Free Church. Secondly, they considered that the measures adopted by the Free Church - having two streams in the Church one availing themselves of the Act and others professedly free - were ineffectual as long as the contract of association had been breached. On a third issue, they differed. For Mr Macfarlane the protest of 1892 had been a legitimate expression of private judgement. It had been recognised in the 1892 Assembly, and the protesters, according to Mr Macfarlane's view, had been given liberty of conscience to safeguard their stance inside the Church, at least until the declaration of 1894 would make precisely clear where the protesters stood. According to the students, the all-important bonds which bound the office-bearer were those which called him to submit to his ecclesiastical superiors - a situation which Mr MacAskill described as a kind of ultramontanism of the Church courts. Where the constitution of the Church had been changed, a person who could not submit to the new rules must protest a⸢ ⸢inst them. Since such a protest, in their view, made it imposs. ⸢e any longer to submit to his ecclesiastical superiors, he was excluding himself from the

Church. The submission of a protest against a binding law was the equivalent of declaring independence from the Church.

Again and again in the period, 1892-93, the students must have reiterated their views that the Declaratory Act had now been passed, and those who, like Mr Macfarlane remained in the Free Church were compromising their position. It was not likely, even though they owed their ordination in 1893 to one of the ministers who stayed in after the Act had been passed in 1892, that they would readily change their views and adopt his. Suffice it to say that articles did appear in which Mr Macfarlane seems to speak with the voice of the students rather than in his own authentic voice. I would suggest that the true voice of Mr Macfarlane is rather to be found in the Answers to Reasons of Dissent of the Abertarff Presbytery or the Kishorn lecture.

In the next chapter I will go on to consider one such particular article.

PART 5: A ROOT OF BITTERNESS

CHAPTER 2

SUBMERGED ROCKS

In volume six of the Free Presbyterian Magazine, in an article by Rev. Donald Beaton the following passage appears:

> "It is true that, according to ecclesiastical procedure, minorities have the right of entering a *dissent* against any legislation to which they have conscientious objections. But, after all, a dissent is of the very mildest form of opposition and it "simply keeps the conscience clear," says Sir Henry Montcrieff, "from the responsibility of what one does not approve of." It, however, by no means nullifies the binding effect of what are termed "binding laws and constitutions." In other words, a dissent relieves the dissentient from all responsibility in the steps leading up to and passing the Act, but it does not relieve him from obligation to obey the Act once it becomes law, provided that Act is of the nature of a binding rule and constitution. That this is the real force of a dissent is pertinently confirmed by Rev. Dr. Mair of Earlston, one of the leading authorities on Church law in the Established Church. "Dissent," he says,

"against the passing of an Act *does not exempt the dissentient from obedience to it,* but relieves him from responsibility for the consequences of the passing of it."

"It is necessary at this stage in our discussion to point out that this (dissenting) is the only course open to minorities in the case of objectionable legislation, and that they have no power to protest against the finding of a Supreme Court unless they are willing to take the steps which persistence in such a course involves, viz., separation from the Church that has passed the law. The greatest confusion exists in the minds of many as to the force of a protest and a dissent. By the bulk they are regarded as implying the same thing. Nothing could be more erroneous and misleading. A dissent may be and is accepted by a Supreme Court against its decisions but never a protest. Such an action would be suicidal. The only time a protest is recognised in Church procedure is before the overture becomes law; and it is worthy of note that Dr Begg, who was such an authority in these matters, always protested before and not after the overture became law. But to make the matter doubly sure, let us again appeal to authorities. Dr. Cook, in his 'Styles of Writs, etc., in the Church of Scotland,' says, 'A dissent can be given in only by those who were present when a judgement dissented from was pronounced, and no protest can be taken against a decision of the Assembly.' Again, Sir Henry Montcrieff, in his 'Practice of the Free Church' says, 'the General Assembly being the Supreme Court, there is no room for any other procedure against its decisions except that of dissent with reasons. There is no room for complaint or appeal.'

"......It only remains for us to take a particular instance wherein these general principles are made manifest. Take the Declaratory Act of 1892, which has caused so much controversy, and has done more than anything else since the Disruption to wreck the ecclesiastical peace of the Highlands. Since that Act passed as an overture through the Barrier Act, and therefore became law, it stands to reason that, by the very terms of the Barrier Act, it became 'a binding rule and constitution,' binding on all the members and judicatories of the Church, to quote Principal Hill's words. It is a fact that will be admitted on all hands that the Constitutional Party considered the doctrines of the Declaratory Act to be of such a nature that nothing short of a protest was sufficient to express their opposition to the same. But what came of these laudable resolutions? In 1893, Rev. Mr Macfarlane tabled his protest, and notwithstanding the efforts made to make him withdraw it, he manfully refused to do so with the result that in a short time he found himself without church or manse. When the Synod of Glenelg felt it its duty to protest against the act its protest was rejected like Mr Macfarlane's with this notable difference, that the members of Synod refused to act on their protest and were content with a dissent. It is therefore only charitable to suppose that those who are declaring throughout the Highlands that they remained in the Free Church under protest, are quite unconscious that there is a world of difference between a protest and a dissent."

It is needless to speak of the worth of Mr Beaton as a minister of the gospel. His name is still savoured by those who knew him for his zeal for the furtherance of the gospel, his broad humanity, his scholarliness as seen in his "Ecclesiastical History of Caithness", his studies of Northern churchmen, his untiring efforts to further the cause that was dearest to him at home and abroad. Nevertheless, I cannot but see his analysis of the 1892-93 period as flawed. Later this analysis was taken as an authoritative exposition of the relation of the Free Presbyterian Church to the Protest of 1893.

1. Because one is dealing with facts, and that is what the events of 1892-93 were by the time Mr Beaton wrote.

Mr Beaton says that the Constitutional Party had said that nothing but a protest would satisfy them in their opposition to the Declaratory Act in 1892. "But what became of these laudable resolutions?" The inference is that they did not protest. On the contrary, they did protest, and in this Mr Macfarlane concurred with them. It is also a fact that that protest did not separate them, since they took an entirely different view of the value of a protest from the view taken by Mr Beaton. The fact that a protest was entered and received at the 1892 Assembly is not mentioned. The same is true of the fact that Mr Macfarlane believed the protest of 1892 at the Assembly gave protection to him and to the protesting minority. Besides, there are implications for Mr Macfarlane's stance that are all but fatal for him if he had only the protection of a dissent from 1892 onward. That dissent would not protect him from obedience to the Act. It is facts like these in relation one to the other that have to be laid out first. Fact should come before theory, and once these facts are fairly laid out, where the theory does not elucidate the facts, the theory must be abandoned and the facts re-examined till a further, more acceptable theory emerges.

2. Mr Beaton says that there cannot be a protest against a law passed through the Barrier Act. He does not consider the exceptional nature of the *contents* of the Act. It is impossible to use a merely procedural Act like the Barrier Act to perform something that is unconstitutional.

a. "All the doctrines of his Act are opposed to the Bible, which is my Word, and the Confession of Faith, which is clearly founded on that Word, and agreeable thereto," says the Judge in the trial of Mr Macfarlane's lecture, "The Declaratory Act in Court." Such an Act might be and, indeed, must be protested against with the same authority that the disciples disobeyed in Acts when they said, "We must obey God and not men."

b. Because of the type of legislation involved. In the presbytery of Abertarff, Mr Macfarlane took the view

> "It is admitted that in the ordinary administration of the Laws of the Church, it is *ultra vires* of an Inferior Court to disobey the orders of a Superior; but the constitution of the Church being mutually agreed upon by all her office-bearers, it is now *ultra vires* of the majority to put their own and a different construction upon that Constitution, as is done by the Declaratory Act."

The Declaratory Act, in other words, changes the relation of the Free Church to the Confession of Faith. It is not said at this point that such an Act could not be passed, provided it is based on a proper view of Scriptural teaching. Nevertheless, the Confession of Faith is the basis of a contract of association. Such a contract cannot lawfully be changed by majority, particularly when the majority give no Scriptural support. Therefore it should not be obeyed, particularly because it leaves the Church at the mercy of succeeding General Assemblies without prior guarantee that they will rule in a Scriptural way.

Mr Beaton's views may, indeed, stand if one is considering the ordinary run of legislation. The Declaratory Act was not ordinary.

3. It is not too much to say that if the statement of Mr Beaton were true, viz. that there was no procedure apart from dissent after a measure passed through the Barrier Act, one of the fundamental bases of the Reformation would be undermined in a church which adopted such a stance. The Reformation is based on Sola Scriptura. That is what provides the element of stability in the Church. The other element is based on the complex of ideas mentioned throughout this book, the headship of Christ, the priesthood of all believers, the existence of the mystical, invisible church owing allegiance to Christ alone, as the bride to the husband, the right of private judgement, the duty of obeying God before men, the right of claiming liberty of conscience within the Church ministerial, the right and duty to oppose implicit faith together with what is clearly contrary to Scripture. The element of Sola Scriptura opposed the Roman Catholic view of Scripture *plus* tradition as the fundamental basis of authority. The other element was "semper reformanda" - always requiring to be reformed - as over against the Roman Church's "semper eadem" - always the same. This element, "semper reformanda", is the element which ensures that the Church never becomes settled on its lees as had happened in the Catholic Church of the Middle Ages.

When one is saying that the Barrier Act ensures that no person can disobey an Act passed under this procedure, one is not speaking of any genuine, innate power in the Barrier Act itself. One is really speaking of the power that a church arrogates to itself if it uses the Barrier Act in this way. Such a church would have forgotten that Christ does not so identify his power with any church that there cannot be appeal beyond the Supreme Court of that church to Him. He would have forgotten the Disruption principle that

> "As the Lord Jesus has appointed a government in His church in the hands of church officers, so we believe, that he has invested the ordinary members of his Church with important spiritual privileges, and has called them to exercise, *on their own responsibility*, important spiritual functions." ("The Engagement", 1840).

He would have forgotten the words of the Confession of Faith that one of these privileges is the right to refuse to make anti-scriptural Acts the rule of practice. He would have forgotten the words of Samuel Rutherford to the effect that the people have the right to reject decrees which are "unsound and false or unjust and wicked." ("Liberty of Conscience.") He would have forgotten that the Church, self-consciously, must bear in mind her obligation to allow divergence of view in such unique cases. He would have forgotten that the stance of Luther, "Here I stand, I can do no other, so help me God," is a stance we would expect to be adopted, not only at the outset of the Reformation Church, but time and again throughout her history, as Christ through His servants speaks to the Church either to redeem her from a backsliding condition or to point out some area of service hitherto disregarded. Only in this way can the watchword, "Semper reformanda," cease to be a mere slogan and become the genuine experience of the Church.

3. The one fact that is mentioned about Mr Macfarlane's action in 1893 tells us nothing, unless the kind of protest that Mr Macfarlane entered in 1893 is specified. Primarily, that protest of 1893 was not a protest against the Act, but a protest in opposition to the Church because they will not allow the protest of the minority. Mr Macfarlane's protest is directly opposed to the precise attitude that Mr Beaton advocates, viz. that there can be no protest against a measure passed through the terms of the

Barrier Act. Mr Macfarlane sees the protesting minority as the "disobedient" remnant who are still obedient to Christ, which can yet bring hope to the Church. He calls on the Church, not with anathemas to expel those who would correct her, as might well happen in a Church which thought of church power flowing to the individual through the stated courts of the Church, but to acknowledge the justice of their stance as should be the case where the headship of Christ links every member with Himself.

The whole protesting procedure of Mr Macfarlane from 1892 to 1893, and with it the emphasis by Mr Macfarlane on the above Refomation principle, is ignored.

Conversely, the facts of Mr Macfarlane's separation fit these principles advocated consistently by him throughout. They cannot be made to fit the views propounded by Mr Beaton.

4. A fourth objection to Mr Beaton's stance is that it would take from Mr Macfarlane the principles of the Evangelicals of the 19th Century - headship of Christ, private judgement, liberty of conscience, opposition to the enforcement of implicit faith. It was on the basis of these principles that he protested in 1892 and stayed in. When he separated in 1893 it was because these principles were denied, not because a protest in itself causes separation. On the other hand, Mr Beaton's opinions would be applauded by the Moderates. From the Moderate Manifesto we can see the right of dissent allowed ......

> "We think it very consistent with conscience for inferiors to disapprove in their own mind of a judgement given by a superior court, and yet to put that judgement in execution, as the deed of their superiors, for conscience sake; seeing we humbly conceive it is, or ought to be, a matter of conscience with every member of the church to support the authority of that church to which he belongs."

.... while the right of protest, on the other hand, is denied;

> "It is very evident that unless the church were
> supported by continual miracles, and a perpetual and
> extraordinary interposition of heaven, it can only
> subsist by those fundamental maxims by which all
> society subsists. A kingdom divided against itself
> cannot stand."

The same arguments already used against this stance of the
Moderates are relevant against Mr Beaton's stance.

5. A fifth objection is that he would have lost the right to say he
followed on Disruption principles. These were exactly the same
as those of the Evangelicals from which this party sprang. The
Church claimed the right to private judgement in interpreting the
power of the Patronage Act to bind them. In the name of the
Head of the Church they refused obedience, and expected to be
given liberty of conscience to act accordingly. The protest of
1842 was not a means of separation any more that the 1892
protest was. It was an appeal to the Head of the Church, on the
basis of the teaching of Scripture saying that obedience to the
terms of the Patronage Act could not be given except in a
qualified way, i.e. only in such a way that would allow them
absolutely to disobey what offended their consciences. In the
same way, in 1892, the Constitutional Party appealed to the head
of the Church that they would not be subject to the terms of the
Declaratory Act.

6. It is equally important that the separation be seen clearly in the
light of Mr Macfarlane's own words, because his actions in the
intervening time, 1892-93, can only be seen in their true light if
this is done. One of the standard accusations which are laid at
Mr Macfarlane's door is that he renewed his vows in this year
when he moved from Kilmallie to Raasay. Indeed, Rev. Neil
Cameron, Glasgow, and in this he is true to the views of the
students over this period, says that he could not understand the
move of Mr Macfarlane. ("It is more than probable, I

understand, that Mr Macfarlane will accept the call to Raasay. If he will he cannot break off at the Assembly according to his public declaration." From private letter of Mr Cameron). If the Declaratory Act had been passed in 1892, reasons Mr Cameron, he took vows under the Declaratory Act, since a protest was, at best, invalid, and the dissent did not secure from obedience to the Declaratory Act. If, on the other hand, as Mr Macfarlane says in "The Declaratory Act in Court," the Act was under review by the Court of heaven over this period, and hence the Free Church ceased to be the true representative of the Free Church only in 1893, when the right of protest was refused, there was no compromise involved. In his correspondance with Rev. Professor Kennedy Cameron, mentioned earlier, Mr Macfarlane said he had entered a protest at the kirk session level, and this had protected him. This is a very different view from that of Mr Cameron. At the same time it was only one aspect, though the most personal aspect, of the protesting movement as it affected him. Only when seen in its full extent as a protest of a whole movement, (the "protesting minority" of the 1893 Assembly protest of Mr Macfarlane), and taking in Assembly, Presbytery and Kirk session can the full effect of the protest be assessed.

7. The most grave charge against Mr Macfarlane that can be made over this period, and it has been made time and again, is that of schism. This has already been touched on at the beginning of this book. At its simplest, it is that if there was no compromise in waiting over one year, 1892 to 1893, there would be no compromise in waiting over the seven years till 1900. The only answer that can be given on the basis of the above analysis by Mr Beaton is that Mr Macfarlane had gauged that by 1893, the situation was clearly hopeless, and therefore he left that year by submitting his protest. No case can be made out that he was not under the Act for that year. If dissent is the only way the Declaratory Act can be opposed, and dissent obligates to obedience, then Mr Macfarlane was subject to the terms of the Declaratory Act without dubiety. The Free Presbyterian Church

remains open to such jibes as those of the correspondent who asked, (Northern Chronicle, Nov. 20, 1901) if the Free Church had rescinded the Declaratory Act, should not the Free Presbyterian have done so also? One year's compromise was as serious as seven year's. Likewise Professor J. Kennedy Cameron says in a letter in July, 1923,

> "The statements I made in that book are that the friends that formed the Free Presbyterian Church remained in full fellowship with the Free Church for a year after the Declaratory Act was passed, and that during that year, Mr Macfarlane was inducted into the Free Church congregation of Raasay. These are historical facts which Mr Macfarlane does not deny. What he maintains, however, is that his protests and statements protected him from complicity in the wrong-doing of the Church in passing such legislation. If this was so in his case, were not the dissents and protests of the minority who remained in the Church equally valid in protecting them? This Mr Macfarlane appears to disallow."

Of course, Mr Macfarlane disallows this. What was distinctive about the protest in 1892 was that it was a protest after the Act had been passed. The protests which the Constitutional Party continued to present after 1892 were merely protests that in entering into discussion about the Declaratory Act, they were not to be understood as admitting "the lawfulness of altering the relation of this Church to any part of its received doctrines, as set forth in its authorised standards, or in terms of subscription thereto." These protests were presented before the various overtures for the rescinding of the Act were presented, and are compatible with the presentation of a dissent after refusal to rescind. Never after 1892 was there a protest following on the refusal to rescind saying that the Act would not be binding on them. These protests ceased with the presentation and refusal of

Mr Macfarlane's protest in 1893. If the Constitutionalists had acted in accordance with their insistence that a protest be received after the Declaratory Act was brought in, as took place in 1892, they would have departed with Mr Macfarlane when he found himself forced into separation in 1893.

In the debate that followed 1938, a protest came to be thought of as an instrument of separation. It was so because a minister would face a charge of violating his ordination vows or of renouncing the jurisdiction of the court if he protested. There is no way by which the claim that a protest is an instrument of separation can be made to fit the unfolding of events in 1892-93. If a protest is an instrument of separation, as it came to be called, then that separation should have taken place when the first protest was presented in 1892. If a protest is a means of preserving one's stance against a call to blind obedience, then both 1892 and 1893 protests can be understood, and Mr Macfarlane's position is preserved. Otherwise, there is no answer to Professor Cameron's accusations.

8. So far as the authorities quoted by Mr Beaton are concerned, Dr Cook was a moderate, and it is not surprising that he should have taken the stance that he did.

So far as Sir Henry Montcrieff is concerned, who says there is no room for complaint or appeal, it is evident he, being a Free Churchman, and hence finding himself on the opposite side of the divide in 1843 from Dr Cook, cannot be so summarily dismissed. The quotation, however, is not complete. Sir Henry Montcrieff goes on to say, "By dissenting with reasons, a man keeps his conscience clear from the responsibility of what he does not approve of. And His appeal goes up to the Head of the Church on high."

There might be debate as to what that last part means. Fortunately, here we are, as mentioned before, dealing with a concrete situation. In 1892, Mr Macfarlane puts beyond doubt what it meant for him. The right of appeal meant that the Consititutional Party could protest against the decision taken at the Assembly and pending the decision of the appeal, take their rightful place in the courts of the Free Church refusing obedience to the Act protested against.

Mr Macfarlane was not alone in considering that disobedience might be rendered to a church court following appeal to the court of heaven. Dr Cunningham in speaking of the sentence of deposition on the Strathbogie ministers says,

> "Now, with respect to the ... administering ordinances when under a sentence of suspension, it is admitted that it is not necessarily, in all cases, an act of direct sin against Christ, because the sentence of suspension may have been erroneously pronounced. It may have been a sentence pronounced *clave errante*, and therefore it is possible they might have acted as they have done in this respect without having committed a sin against the Lord Jesus Christ, provided they had appealed to Christ on conscientious grounds against the sentence of the Church. Only on this understanding would they have been justified in disregarding the sentence of their ecclesiastical superiors."

The quotation about Dr Begg is lifted out of a speech made by Dr Rainy in 1893. It refers to the union controversy of 1863-73. Dr Begg regularly protested after resolutions had been carried in the Assembly, but since the Union negotiations never came to a decisive climax, he never protested after the final deliverance of the Assembly since it never did come in fact to a final conclusion. Nevertheless, he made abundantly clear that he would have protested in such an eventuality after the decision. Thus, the actions of Dr Begg can, in fact, be pleaded in support of the

Constitutional protest in 1892, and the right to continue that protest in 1893. Indeed, as Mr MacAskill said, the Declaratory Act was not complete till 1894. If Dr Begg's actions be taken as a precedent, then the right of protest should be sustained after all resolutions up to that point.

It is simply impossible to impose the view that a protest cannot be received and must result in separation upon such   a construction of events as Mr Macfarlane outlines in "The Declaratory Act in Court." There, there are three clear phases.

1. The Declaratory Act is finally agreed to by the courts of the Free Church.

2. The protest entered at that time together with the appeal to the court of heaven suspends the Act, and allows time for trial by the heavenly court.

3. Though judgement is made by the heavenly court in favour of those who adhered to the Confession of Faith, the majority who had passed the Declaratory Act refused to change the decision come to at the preceding Assembly. The minority protested against the arrogance of the majority which attempted to make the minority accept their views; (protested at the overriding of their rights of protest). They were forced into separation.

The attempt to derive from this that a protest cannot be received is doomed to failure. It should never have been made.

This view, that a protest separated the protester, lay like a submerged reef just below the surface. Given the possibility of a person presenting a protest, there could be a ship-wreck.

PART 5: A ROOT OF BITTERNESS

CHAPTER 3

REV. EWAN MACQUEEN OF CAMASTIANAVAIG

Rev. Ewan Macqueen could be described, had the word attained its present usage while he lived, a "charismatic" personality. As is the hap with such characters, it is often trivial, ideosyncratic events they are remembered for and the depths of their concern is forgotten. Here are two such trivia. He was born in Camastianavaig, a hamlet in the Braes district of Skye. Highland hamlets often share with Welsh hamlets the characteristic of having a size in inverse proportion to their population. Mr Macqueen himself played on this, it is said, when passing through the customs between Canada and the USA. "Where do you come from?" asked the official. "From Camastianavaig," said Mr Macqueen. "And where is Camastianavaig?" asked the official. "Why, your geography has been sadly neglected," countered Mr Macqueen.

There is a kind of defensive mechanism in the Highland character, as in the character of all minorities. Sometimes it shows itself in the bravado of Mr Macqueen illustrated above. The humour of the above situation would probably be lost on an Englishman since it depends on knowing the insecurity of being part of a minority. The same defensive mechanism is seen in the other direction. Humour can be made out of the characteristics of the minority itself, and situations defused in this way. Perhaps this is the origin of another story which was told of Mr Macqueen. It was said he was in a London shop, and wished to buy a pair of pyjamas. His Highland drawl was so pronounced that the attendant could make out nothing of what Mr Macqueen was saying. A "guide, counsellor and friend", probably from the local congregation, accompanied Mr Macqueen, and eventually the attendant turned to him and said, "What is the gentleman saying?" By this time so embarassed was Mr Macqueen's companion that when he tried to pronounce the word in best Oxford English the result was no more comprehensible than Mr Macqueen's own attempts.

Mr Macqueen began his ministry in Dornoch, and in an obituary of Angus Gray, a local worthy, he shows how he must have felt totally at one with such men. The obituary rolls straight into a description of the conversion of Angus. It was through a sermon of Dr Kennedy, Dingwall, that his conversion took place. "His words came into my heart like balls of fire, inflaming it with love to the person of whom he spake." He went home, says Mr Macqueen, but not to sleep. "All night he felt, as he would say, that Christ was like a mountain of fire burning with love before his mind, and that although seven lakes of fire lay between him and the children of men, he would wade through them all to be in His bosom."

Mr Macqueen, himself, did not lack a knowledge of that love, nor of a desire to impart that love to others. Here is a description of seeing a detachment of Lovat Scouts leave Bedford.

"On coming to the street it was clear that something new was happening for all the town seemed alive. Then I heard the bagpipes which appeals to all Highlanders, but any life which the bagpipes may have stirred up in my

Highland nature, soon died away when I saw so many of my dear countrymen on the move for the field of gore. Some of them shook hands with me in passing, and as the last of them passed by, I felt my heart going from me and following the dear men who were willingly marching, some of them to their doom, in defence of their king and Country. For a time I stood staring after them, desiring that the Lord would speed the day when the nations shall learn war no more, when proud sin shall hide its face for very shame."

By this time, Mr Macqueen had been inducted in Kames, Argyll-shire. Having been brought up in Kames, I well remember some of the stories recounted by Donald McPherson, an elder there, who had known Mr Macqueen's ministry in his youth. While clipping the hedge in the front garden, he spied a man who had not been attending his ministry as regularly as Mr Macqueen thought he should have been. He asked him the reason why, to which he received the rejoinder that he would come when the gospel really was free. The first thing that met his gaze when he entered the church was a collection plate. This fact hardly tallied with the claimed freedom of the gospel.
A few weeks after that, the man made one of his infrequent appearances. Mr Macqueen singled him out in the congregation, telling of what had passed between them. "If you want free water," he said, "Go up into the lochs at the back of Kames and you will have abundance. If you want it piped into you back-kitchen, you must pay water-rates - not for the water but for the service. The same is true with the gospel."

It is little wonder, expressing as he does in the above quotation such great interest in the lives of the soldiers at this time serving in the First World War in France, that before long he became a chaplain in

France, sharing in their privations. "We used to say on the West of Scotland, when one heard a certain person praised, 'You did not burn a peat-stack with him yet.' I may say about them - the more I knew them, the more I loved them."

In an address delivered in Glasgow in 1916, and reported in the Free Presbyterian Magazine, though doubtless an off-the-cuff report, one gains an idea of what made Mr Macqueen so attractive a preacher. He never lacks variety. There is first the punch.

> "We may speak about the expanse of the Atlantic, but I will tell you something that is more extensive and more expansive than even the Atlantic; it is the greed that is in the human heart. .... and I may say that this has been the cause of the aweful War in which we are engaged at the present moment, greed in the heart."

There are snippets of personal experience, perhaps not without a touch of hyperbole.

> "We have to get a needle pressed into our breast now and again. A man comes along with a long needle, and asks you to open up your breast, and when you do so, he stabs the needle into your breast. It won't do to say, 'You must not put it there.' The stuff put in is rank poison, as people would say in Skye, but that rank poison is there to counteract or keep away enteric fever."

There are insights into his own personal spiritual life.

> "They call the ministers, Padrays, and, of course, Padray Macqueen had to be out at half past six as well as the rest. Then when we turned out in the morning, the first thing was to wash our bodies, and to dress for the duties of the day. And, friends, whenever we had this done,

the man who had a mind for an hour in private with the
Most High, that was the time he got for it."

There are insights into how he got a hearing for himself, and not
without some guile in the process.

"As they lay there on stretchers, whatever pain they had,
unless they had sickness, they all liked 'a smoke,' and
those who were much wounded, 'longed' as they said
themselves, 'for a cigarette'. If you went in with a
bundle of 'Wills' Wild Woodbine' you would get a smile
on everyone's face." "At other times I would go out in
search of the Highlanders - for although I love the
Lowlanders, I must say I have a warm place in my heart
for the poor Highlanders - when I would come in sight
of 'the kilties' and hear their old musical instrument, the
bagpipes, I used to feel: 'I am coming near those that I
love the most. I am coming near the Highlanders.'
Sometimes I would not have a very long time, and I
would ask them in Gaelic, 'If I would come and give a
kind of sermon to you, would you come to hear me?' and
they would say, 'It is we that would be pleased to see
you and hear you, sir.' "

There is the "cianalas", (home-sickness) for home.

"As I was drawing near the time when I was to get leave
- you see, a soldier is a soldier - the last fortnight before
I got leave I felt longer than the two months and a half
previous to that, because I have a human heart, I hope,
and my heart longed to see my dear family once more in
the land of the living, and as my heart longed to see my
dear family, my heart longed to speak once more to my
own congregation. But the week before I got away,
word came stopping all leave, and I can tell you I had to

go on my knees to seek submission from God, if I
should be kept back. For you know there is a rebellious
heart inside, and when I had made up my mind to see
my friends, the old rebellion was ready to come to life
again. But at the very last moment, word came round
that I would get home on special leave."

That address, of course, is hardly a sermon. Mr Macqueen, himself,
calls it a "rigmarole". The elements of racy presentation, of
personal anecdote, of earnest and loving application are there, and it
is these elements that linger on in the memory of those who heard
him preach.

Three months later he is back in France.

"I am giving Bibles away continually and other books.
Our work grows here every day. I had a meeting last
night where we had hundreds of men who not only gave
the outward ear, but also listened with interest to what
was said to them, and while others were away at a
boxing match, they were content listening to the Word of
God."

There are a number of ways his time in France must have marked
Mr Macqueen. He had to serve, not only all Scottish Presbyterians
in the unit in which he was based, but English dissenters as well.
This doubtless gave a much more ecumenical cast to his subsequent
ministry. He used to come to Elphin every year and preach for the
Church of Scotland minister there. One lady who lived in the hills
made a yearly pilgrimage to hear him. To a young girl who
wondered what the fuss was, her father said simply, Mr Macqueen
preaches the gospel. She was one of the many young persons in the

course of Mr Macqueen's ministry, who, finding it impossible to remain at rest the length of the service, was promised a sweetie from the pulpit if she would remain quiet till the conclusion.

Many other quaint anecdotes are told of Mr Macqueen. Some are, perhaps, more revealing than quaint, showing a very human personality in his defects as truly as in his virtues.

Latterly, he moved to Inverness. He found himself in two situations of difficulty, and they may have both been not a little influenced by the army days. Since my interest is not in the proceedings of the courts in relation to these matters, I will severely leave them alone and come to the point which alone is relevant to the theme of this book.

The Synod in 1938 found against Mr Macqueen in one of these cases. When the decision was announced, Rev. Ewan Macqueen stood, read, and tabled this Protest: "To the Synod of the Free Presbyterian Church of Scotland met at Inverness, this 29th day of June, 1938, I protest against your finding because I consider it to be irregular, unconstitutional and unscriptural."

"The moderator warned Mr Macqueen of the grave nature of his action, that it meant that he was separating himself from the Free Presbyterian Church of Scotland.... Continuing firm in his attitude, he left the Synod. When he had gone, the moderator, Rev. Donald Beaton, intimated that Mr Macqueen's name would be removed from the Roll of the Northern Presbytery, his charge must be declared vacant, and his salary would cease from that day." ("Free Presbyterian History.")

At this late date, is it not pointless to attempt to defend the decision in the Macqueen case of 1938? The ground has thoroughly been gone over in the Inverness Manse Case of 1951. No persuasive precedents could be produced to show that a protest separated a person. The most that can be said is that such a person, if he continues holding to his protest, would be arraigned on a charge of contumacy, and if this contumacy continued would face suspension or even deposition. The real reason for holding so rigidly to the rightness of the decision, and the Free Presbyterian Church has never even reconsidered it in spite of defeat in this case, is the view that even to question it would undermine Mr Macfarlane's own stance. I will develop this view in the next chapter.

PART 5: A ROOT OF BITTERNESS.

CHAPTER 4

"ASK NOT FOR WHOM THE BELL TOLLS"

The position of the Free Presbyterian Church on protest can be outlined as follows.

No conscientious disobedience is allowed after the final Act of the Supreme Court.

Dissent does not involve disobedience. It is therefore allowed after the final act of the Supreme Court of the Church; dissent simply absolves from any responsibility in relation to the passing of an Act. The dissenter cannot argue from the mere fact of tabling his dissent and the reception of that dissent by the Court, that he is free from the obligation to submit to the Act once that Act has been passed.

Protest is the equivalent stance to that of the disciples in Acts of the Apostles when they said, "We must obey God rather than men." Freedom from responsibility for passing the Act in question by a court of which he is a member - which he could gain by registering a dissent - is not enough for one adopting a protesting stance. He looks into the future and says, however much he may agree with all other stances of the particular church in which he finds his lot, "I cannot conscientiously submit to this particular measure."

The merest possibility that a protest might be admitted by a Supreme Court is judged incompatible with the requirements of the ordination vows. Since the ordination vows, (it is alleged), require complete obedience to the courts of the Church, any protest after an Act becomes law means that the protester cannot remain any longer in the particular Church of which he is an office-bearer. Indeed, the protest, itself, carries him "beyond the pale." The courts cannot tolerate disobedience.

So far as the passage of the Declaratory Act in 1892 was concerned, the Church was placed in a dilemma. It was faced with the difficulty that Mr Macfarlane stayed in after the Declaratory Act had been passed in 1892. By reason of its anti-Scriptural nature, Mr Macfarlane had made it abundantly clear that he would not submit to the Declaratory Act. He cited as the basis of the right to remain within the Free Church the fact that there was a protesting minority in the Church of which he, as a protester, was an integral part. So far from being expelled from the Church by their protest, they were actually protected by it. In assessing the separation of 1893, the Free Presbyterian Church attempted to be faithful both to the stance of Mr Macfarlane and to their view that a protest would separate. Hence they ignored, or at least played down, the entry of a protest in 1892, saying that since Mr Macfarlane was not present in the Assembly in 1892, he could stand at a distance, so far as responsibility was concerned, from the passage of the Declaratory Act in that year. The official history says that there was a clause in the protest saying that there would be an attempt to have the Declaratory Act rescinded in 1893. (There was, in fact, no such clause). They then highlighted the protest of 1893, as though at this Assembly Mr Macfarlane first entered into the fray in earnest. They claimed that the protest of Mr Macfarlane, being a refusal to "act under what had now been made law in the Church" separated Mr Macfarlane since no-one can sustain such a stance within a Church. The fact was ignored that Mr Macfarlane had not been acting under what had been made law in 1892 for a whole year already. The actual terms of the 1893 protest have never been thought important enough to expound. The word, "protest", and the fact that Mr Macfarlane tabled the protest, resolutely refusing to withdraw it when pressed to do so, is sufficient, given their view of protest, to indicate that Mr Macfarlane separated himself by his 1893 protest.

In the previous pages I have sought to put a different construction on the separation of 1893. Mr Macfarlane was carried into separation, not because a protest inevitably means separation, but because the rights of such a protest which were allowed in 1892, and which protected him over the period, 1892-93, in the Assembly of 1893 were taken away.

If there were any doubt about the connection between the protest of Mr Macqueen, spoken of in last chapter, and the way it was dealt with, and the protest of Mr Macfarlane in 1893, that connection is put beyond question by the words of Rev. Donald Beaton in a statement in 1943. "Some may ask, however, what connection has the protest tendered by Mr Macqueen in 1938 with the protest of 1893 tabled by Mr Macfarlane? The answer to this can be given in a few words. The Synod in 1938 were guided by the view always held among us that the protest of 1893 effectually separated Mr Macfarlane from the Declaratory Act Church."

Mr Beaton then goes on to two further points. He says that it was a protest that separated the Free Church from the Establishment in 1843. This could only be relevant if this was the first protest in which the majority in the church of Scotland at that time were involved. Only then can it be said that the protest, *per se*, caused separation. It was not the first protest. There was a protest the previous year. This did not cause separation, nor was it meant to cause separation even though it indicated refusal to submit to the Patronage Act. Hence, far from proving that a protest indicating refusal to submit on conscientious grounds brings about separation, it shows that it is rather a plea to the superior ruling authority, in this case the state, to yield to the headship of Christ.

The other is a quotation from Dr Rainy, which cannot surely carry weight by way of shedding any light on Mr Macfarlane's opinions, since Dr Rainy clearly opposed the stance of Mr Macfarlane on protest. Dr Rainy believed the Declaratory Act should stand and the protest fall. Mr Macfarlane believed the Act should fall and the protest stand. At a later point in his statement, Mr Beaton quoted the article in vol. 6 of the magazine to show that he had consistently held the same views down through the years.

If the views expressed in the article in volume six of the magazine lie at the basis of the decision in 1938, as Mr Beaton says they do, I cannot see, in all humility, that the decision of Synod that Mr Macqueen separated himself by his protest is either safe or satisfactory.

Rev. R. Mackenzie, Glasgow, took up the matter of protest and issued a pamphlet in which he said that he had been contending against two views (1) that a protest tabled against the Supreme Court of a Church necessarily means and effects separation from the Church and (2) that in the case of an office-bearer such tabling of a protest necessarily involves the violation of an ordination promise. According to the argument I have followed so far, Mr Mackenzie was right on both counts. A protest that is registered with a Supreme Court accompanied with an appeal to the Court of heaven would defeat its own purpose if it meant separation. Its aim is to have an effect on that Supreme Court, leading, it is hoped, to the withdrawal or modification of the offending legislation, and separation would mean the loss of all influence in this direction. It can only be assessed as a violation of an ordination promise to be subject to the Courts of the Church if these courts will not allow such protest. Only then will the protester be in a stance of contumacy. I have argued that any right thinking Supreme Court will allow protest when properly presented, on a suitable topic and on tenable grounds. According to Principal Cunningham, men may appeal to Christ on conscientious grounds against a decision, even when the Supreme Court is acting as a court of review.

Mr Mackenzie was told he would have to retract his opinions or leave in six months. Inevitably, he was forced into separation since affairs were at an impasse when this motion had been made and in the intervening six months, no new evidence was presented.

From 1971 to 1978 I attempted to raise the matter at the Synod. My petitions were not received. In 1978, my mouth was finally closed. I suppose I could write a book on the efforts I have made to bring attention to these issues in the courts of the FP Church, - a book that would doubtless be much more flavourful than the one I am currently writing - but I must not do so. It is inevitable that when involved in controversial issues, those who stand outside and cannot see the internal motivation of the person concerned are not slow to search for and find reasons why an individual takes up a particular stance. One of the Covenanters once prayed, "The travail of Christ's soul, let it be mine." To me, the divisions that had been caused by the issues I have outlined above were part of the travail of Christ's soul. I could not divorce myself from them if love to Jesus Christ was one of the prime aims of my ministry. If I were now to enter into the fray on the level of attempting to clear my name or to "get even" with those who have imputed less than honourable motives to me in what I strove to achieve, it would at the very least give credence to a suspicion that it was a personal rather than a spiritual impulse that directed me, and would mean that the principles that I have attempted to set out would be so far obscured.

Since the 1978 ruling was considered to be the ruling to end all rulings on the topic of protest, let me say why I could not be satisfied with it.

1. The Synod said that issues relating to protest were "of a procedural character and not of a substantive character affecting the constitution of the Church." However this statement may be justified, the relevant point so far as the particular case I highlighted, that of 1892-1893, was that neither party considered protests to be merely procedural. Mr MacAskill, according to the letter to "The Scotsman", and Mr Macfarlane, according to his Kishorn lecture, thought their protests were expressions of liberty of conscience which were admissible because of the unique headship of Christ over the Church. The students, who formed another and opposing stance within the Free Presbyterian Church did not think protests were merely procedural, either, since the presentation of protests contravened ordination vows. This goes beyond a merely procedural indication of a wish to separate.

2. I was asked "to desist from further agitating the minds of our loyal people with discussion of these questions." Considering the turmoil these questions created within my own mind, I would have been heartily glad to desist. My situation was somewhat akin to two sisters by the name of Misses Black in Halkirk, Caithness, with whom my brother was once staying while supplying the congregation at the week-end. He had dropped off to sleep in his room, and was still slumbering when the evening service was coming perilously close. Eventually the Misses Black aroused him, and he heard in the background when they had retreated after the accomplishment of their mission, "We didn't want to disturb him, but it was disturbing he needed." The Free Presbyterian Church needed disturbing, and it was in the name of loyalty to her fundamental stance this had to be done. The loyal people in my view were not those who did not question, but such as raised very valid and timely questions.

3. I was told to give myself to the "vital and ordinary duties" of my ministerial office. This doubtless meant the duty to call my local congregation to "repentance towards God and faith in our Lord Jesus Christ." Why should this preclude calling the Free

Presbyterian Church to repentance and faith when I perceived they were not acting correctly? Was this not a vital and ordinary duty? In churches which have a hierarchy, a case could be made out for leaving issues of church correction as over against individual correction to bishops and archbishops. At the same time, the principle, itself, that the Church should submit herself to self-criticism is clear. Whence, then, must correction come? Presbyterian churches have no exalted ranks of clergy, charged with a general oversight over the church, and if correction is to come about it must begin with the humble presbyter. The whole Bible witnesses to the need for the Church to "judge herself that she should not be judged." Isaiah preaches, indeed, against the foreign nations with their idolatry, and against those within the confines of the land of promise who do not act according to the law, such as the drunkards of Ephraim. He equally preaches against those who keep fast days and solemn assemblies while issues of practical morality are not being addressed. That was precisely the case as I saw it. If Mr Macfarlane's separation was to be seen in its proper light, if the charges of schism were to be resisted, if sections within and without the Free Presbyterian Church who had been alienated were to be restored, the Church had to let in the thought, with all the agitation that accompanied it, that it might have been wrong. Jeremiah's message was rejected because he was agitating the minds of the loyal people of the land in his time with the thought that Israel's sin lay at the basis of the seige of Jerusalem. As he saw it, the matter must be done. It was a matter of vital and ordinary duty.

4. It is curious that the very principles for which I was contending were embodied in the Overture presented to the Synod in 1989 by which Mr Murray justifies the action taken by him and Lord Mackay in that year. I hope to show this before the end of this book. Yet these principles which I considered underlay the protest of Mr Macfarlane were in 1978 considered dangerous even to breathe in the public arena.

Why did the Free Presbyterian Church not allow discussion of these matters publicly? (In the 1978 case, after years of not being given even the opportunity to make a speech, I was given fifteen minutes. The speech was not recorded in the Synod Proceedings, nor even the motion against which I had appealed.) Doubtless there was a presumption that those who had gone before, who had actually been present in 1893, and had left on record their views, were right, and that such as myself who had come so lately on the scene could not possibly have an understanding not professed before my time. Both at Synod and at presbytery I was charged with claiming to bring in new light, as though that itself were a crime. At the same time, I could sense an underlying reason which reached no higher than the reasons why political parties are so loathe to admit to failings in their policies. It is the matter of image. The moment grave faults in the past are admitted, both to the constituency of the people of the Free Presbyterian Church, and to sister (and rival) churches, the Church is seen to be less than perfect. A church that is less than perfect cannot claim, it is assumed, the same loyalty from her people. When there are other runners in the race, claiming to be the true, original Reformed Church of Scotland, it may be that the palm will be conceded to them. Hence, at all events, the church must not admit fault.

How such a view fails totally to assess where the true strength of a church lies! The headship of Christ over the church means that it is in her weakness her strength is made perfect. David was at his weakest when claiming, in response to the parable told him by Nathan about the wealthy man who stole the lamb from the poor man, to be a fit judge in such matters, free from any such guilt of his own. He was at his strongest when in full and free confession he said, "My sin is ever before me", and when he threw himself on the mercy of God, "Have mercy upon me O God, according to thy lovingkindness: according unto the multitude of thy tender mercies blot out my transgressions." Peter was at his weakest when he said, "Though all should deny thee, yet shall not I". He was at his strongest when, having confessed his sin, he pointed to Christ on the Day of Pentecost, or in the presence of the Jewish council, saying, He is exalted "a Prince and a Saviour, to give repentance to Israel and forgiveness of sins."

My Free Presbyterian minister friend on the Isle of Skye, brought up a refrain common in Free Presbyterian circles. "The Spirit of God is denied today." The inference is that since iniquity abounds, there can be little prospect of the furtherance of the gospel until foundations that have been lost are restored. God is grieved, and this has its effect on those who preach sound doctrine. The only option is to wait till the inevitable denouement - what the Old Testament prophets would call "the Day of the Lord" - when men will see the folly of their trust in "vanity and lies" and turn back to the Truth. The implication is that only in the world "out there" is defection to be detected. What if I were to suggest that defection may be much more close to home?

The APC has been little more receptive to my views than the Free Presbyterian Church was. In the one case when I took up the matter formally, I was given fifteen minutes to speak. I cannot now mention the matter in church courts without arousing a response of hilarity. However, there are two distinct advantages I have now. The APC have allowed me permission to print, a permission which I am now taking advantage of, without the certainty of disciplinary proceedings. This is the situation I was under in the Free Presbyterian Church. Besides, I think I can show before I finish that the very issues I was contending for in 1978 were the issues that the APC contended for at its inception.

Finally, I have already mentioned the reference to me in John McLeod's book, "No Great Mischief if you Fall". At an earlier point, after saying some kindly things about me, he says that I was chronically unable to discipline my talents. "he lacked concentration, and one must say that this owed something to dreadful ill-health - he had been one of Scotland's first kidney transplant patients, in November, 1969, and has been for some years the senior transplant survivor in Scotland. But he yet had liver trouble, heart trouble, and a host of other troubles. When I last heard of Fraser Tallach, he had just broken his heel."

I hasten to say that his report of my liver trouble is quite inaccurate. Liver trouble has certain unfortunate associations in the Highlands. The rest is true, though I would hardly describe my troubles as "a host", and I cannot say whether I am the oldest transplant patient in Scotland or not. Nevertheless, I would be loathe to think that any of the medical staff who, in a variety of ways and places I have been deeply indebted to for their services, would consider that the only result of any public note that has been gained from their efforts to keep me alive has been that I "foolishly chose to immerse myself in the Charybdis of the Protest controversy." If what I have written in this book does not speak for me in this regard, nothing else will.

Subsequently Revs. Brentnall and Radcliff brought up the issue of protest before the Synod. Their view on protest can be gathered from the first plea of their overture. It was that the Synod "rule that a Protest made against a decision of the Supreme Court of the Church does not of itself separate the protester from the Church." They were not allowed to speak on the substance of their overture and since they would not promise not to spread their views of protest, they were first suspended for a year in 1980 and *sine die* in 1981.

If the contention I have argued for on the basis of Mr Macfarlane's own words is accepted, i.e. that a protest in 1892 was considered to be the accompaniment of an appeal to the Court of heaven; if it is agreed that it is an action embodying the rights of private judgement and liberty of conscience; if it is agreed that such a protest may be received, and when received, gives the protester not only exemption from the responsibility of being a party to the passing of the Act protested against, but also protection from the application of the Act to him; if it is agreed that only when the right of protest is denied does it leave the protester with no alternative but to separate, then three things follow:

1. There was no need for the separation of Mr Mackenzie and his followers.

2. There was no need for the separation of Messrs. Brentnall and Radcliff.

3. The Free Presbyterian Church are seen right up to their latest ruling on the matter consistently following the line of the students in 1892 who believed that ordination vows gave no place to the exercise of private opinion and liberty of conscience of the kind displayed above.

PART 6: THE PRESENT FREE CHURCH

CHAPTER 1

THE DEMISE OF A LEADER

The editorial leader in "The Northern Chronicle" for September 7th, 1892 begins as follows:

> "The fiery vigour displayed by Mr Macfarlane, Kilmallie, at Flashadder Free Church communion in Skye, ... was in stark contrast with the milk and water resolution come to by the meeting of the Free Church Constitutional Committee held at Inverness on Monday. At that meeting, Mr MacAskill, Dingwall who presided, proposed, we understand, that arrangements should there and then be made for sending deputations to all the Presbyteries and congregations of the Highlands to enlighten the people about the attitude of the party in regard to the Declaratory Act and cognate subjects, and to elicit public opinion. But the majority preferred a motion to delay taking that decided step meantime, and to issue as one pamphlet, five thousand copies of the Declaratory Act in Gaelic, with an explanatory statement, and the resolutions adopted at the

conventions held at Inverness and Glasgow appended. Mr MacAskill, we learn, did not think the issuing of the pamphlet would be of much value...."

Throughout the course of the year between the two Assemblies there was a steady weakening of the stance of Mr Macaskill in relation to the 1892 protest. This must have followed pressure from two fronts. There was pressure from the majority party in the Church. It became clear as the minority party presented their protests at the various presbyteries of the Church, that the protest which had been received at the Assembly would die the death of a thousand cuts. Dr Stalker in the Glasgow presbytery said that they might stop the whole proceedings at the point at which they arrived and they would still have the Declaratory Act, to which anyone who signed the Confession might look, because there were other Declaratory Acts, and everyone who signed the formula was quite aware that he was entitled to these Declaratory Acts in his own mind and conscience. Mr MacAskill's aim was to make a final stand in 1894 according to his speech at the 1892 Assembly. He would not reach 1894 if he insisted on the full force of the protest. He would have to separate in 1893, at the next Assembly. Consider how different Mr MacAskill's tone is in speaking on the protest when seeking to have it entered in the books of his presbytery in September 28, in the next month after his letter to "The Scotsman", and three weeks after the above article.

"Undoubtedly, a protest against any action of the Supreme Court of the Church is a serious thing, and it is truly sad that in such a case as the present it should be necessary. But for such a protest to be unconstitutional depends altogether upon the kind of action against which it is taken and the manner in which the protest itself is expressed. We can easily imagine protests which on the one hand would be useless, and on the other would be inadmissible. To protest, for instance, against the decision of the General Assembly as the final Court of Review, in a case at the bar is useless, and on the face of it, absurd. Again, to table an absolute protest against the validity of a General Assembly in any of its public Acts is plainly inadmissible, because it would be calling in question the supreme and rightful authority of the Court, itself, calling in question, in short, its right to exist, and disowning its authority. The immediate consequence of such action would necessarily be the disowning of and separation from the jurisdiction of such a Court by the protesters. Such was the nature of the action which resulted in the Disruption." (Ross-shire Journal, Sept. 30, 1892)

The specific form of protest which was entered in 1892 was "a protest against the validity of the General Assembly in one of its public acts", viz. the passing of the Declaratory Act. This now is described as inadmissible. A month before he had been speaking of the tyranny of the Assembly; of the fact that the protesters who adhere to the constitution to have a right to oppose the action of the Assembly to the utmost, and to do this in the name of that Scriptural constitution itself, "with its sacred legacy of spiritual rights and liberties". Principle is so strong, that the dire consequences of being forced out of the Church are of little consequence. Now, fear of being forced into a premature separation seems to be uppermost in his mind, and the rights of opposing an unconstitutional act of the Assembly so watered down that the protest is given no more power than a dissent. They must not follow the Disruption Church. Whyever not? Their stance in 1842 was exactly the same as that of the Constitutional Party in 1892. In

1842 conscience would not allow the Evangelicals to administer the Patronage Act so far as admitting ministers into congregations who would not have them. In 1892, conscience would not allow the Constitutional Party to admit the Declaratory Act as binding on them. The next year, 1843, the Evangelical party was forced into separation by the refusal of their protest. Would not the 1892 Constitutional Party have an honourable precedent if, finding their protest refused in 1893, as it had been accepted in 1892, they would with full colours flying quit the vitiated Church which would not give them a home, just as in 1843, Dr Chalmers and his friends quitted the vitiated Establishment. In the August letter, Mr MacAskill teases Mr Robertson that he is afraid of the Slough of Despond, and is determined to retreat. In his own speech at the Presbytery a month later, his greatest fear is that the protesters would go so far that they would disown and separate from the jurisdiction of the General Assembly.

The second pressure on Mr MacAskill is already intimated in the first quotation above. It would seem that his Constitutional fellow-ministers were not agreed on separating in 1894, itself, and were bent on a kind of course of delay till the union actually took place between the Free Church and the United Presbyterian. Over the next few months following this meeting, the division between Mr Macfarlane's stance and that of the main Constitutional Party widened. As the quotation shows, Mr MacAskill was at first a decidedly reluctant fellow-traveller with his fellow Constitutional Party brethren. By the time of the Assembly of 1893 he had come on board. The change in Mr MacAskill's views are seen by the contrast between his statements in 1893, and his statements in 1892. I will go on to consider why this was so.

First, I will summarise his position at the Assembly of 1892, together with the light that his statements directly after 1892 shed on that stance.

In 1892, he considered that the Declaratory Act was not as yet law. It would not become law for two years after that date. He would refuse to ordain ministers who sought to take ordination under the Declaratory Act. When the Declaratory Act had already become the Act of a former General Assembly, how could he do this? He would need, both to keep his own stance clear and to give him leverage to attack the Act when any sought to take refuge under it, to be able to show that it existed at best in a suspended state as yet, at least until 1894. Both these points of vantage he could gain, not by a dissent, but by a protest.

In 1893, Mr MacAskill should still be claiming that the Act is as yet suspended, but when Dr Rainy in an impassioned sally attacks the very position he had adopted last Assembly, Mr MacAskill makes no reply.

> "Now what is proposed? It is said to us that these Presbyteries and kirk sessions will, at their own hand, raise the question of what the secret mind of the individual is with regard to the Declaratory Act ... and they are to refuse to licence or ordain every man who does not there and then disclaim the Declaratory Act ...." (This is precisely what Mr MacAskill said he would do.) "Am I not justified in saying that our sole anxiety on this side is to see that our friends do not oppress other people?"

Even more revealing is the attitude that Mr MacAskill takes to the protest presented by Mr Macfarlane. Mr Macfarlane says that he had approached prominent members of the Constitutional Party at the Assembly, seeking to persuade them to present a protest. They would not do this. Why not? A protest was presented before discussion began in the debate, saying that in entering into the debate, they did not admit the lawfulness of changing bringing in the Declaratory Act. This had been done in 1892 as well. Why was the pattern of 1892 not carried through to its conclusion? Why was a protest not presented at the end, when the Declaratory Act was approved?

Further, when Mr Macfarlane had the courage to present a protest, why does Mr MacAskill say that he "understood that all the force Mr Macfarlane wanted to give to the document was that of a very strong dissent from the act done that day." It is clear as crystal that that is not all the force Mr Macfarlane wanted to give to the document. If there were any dubiety about the passage where he says neither his conscience nor ordination vows would allow him to act under what had been made law, that dubiety is entirely removed when he says he protests against the despotic power used in the suppression of the protesting minority. Dissents had never been suppressed. There was no need to suppress them since they did not set up a rival and opposing stance against the Act.

Why at an earlier debate in the Assembly, when he himself is speaking of the protests that came to the Assembly's notice from the presbyteries of Skye and Lochcarron, does the trumpet give such an uncertain sound?

> "The protests were not protests in the technical sense of that word. They were simply formal declarations that they did not agree to the version of the doctrines of their church given in that Act. Protest in the technical sense could only be against a decision from the bar, or the jurisdiction of the Court else. The first was useless; the

second could result only in separation. They in the Highlands knew perfectly well the result of a protest in either of these aspects against the decision of the General Assembly. Their protests were not given in this sense. They were simply a formal declaration against the Act being imposed upon them, or their being compelled to administer the same."

A "formal declaration that one did not agree to the version of the doctrines given in the Declaratory Act" is a dissent. That does not prevent administration of the Act. As noted above, the contrast between this statement and the letter to "The Scotsman" in August 1892 defending these same Presbytery protests could hardly be more distinct. There he had spoken of the Church having gone beyond the limits of her constitution and of resistance "to the utmost." Now he speaks only of "formal declarations that they did not agree to the versions of the doctrines of their church given in that Act." So far as the Act being imposed upon the protesters was concerned, he knew perfectly well no-one, whether he protested or not, was going to force him to preach the doctrines of the Declaratory Act. On the other hand, he needed to be able to claim freedom from the Act as an office-bearer in such official acts as ordination. In a Church which had agreed to the terms of the Act, he needed more than a mere gesture of defiance on the books of presbytery. He needed a protest of the strength Mr Macfarlane presented saying that he would not act under the Act.

At the 1892 Assembly he had spoken of bringing those who would not dissociate themselves from the Declaratory Act before the Assembly. Now he says the protest is simply "a formal declaration against .... their being compelled to administer the same." In 1892, he was very conscious that without aggressive opposition they would, willy nilly, be operating the Act. Now he speaks as though the mere existence of formal declarations on the books of presbyteries was sufficient to preserve their consciences.

Then he had spoken of separation as though almost welcoming the prospect.

> "To that Scriptural constitution, with its sacred legacy of spiritual rights and liberties the Constitutional Party will strictly adhere, disregarding alike the sneers of tyranny of their opponents, and the defection of some of their weak-kneed friends. They will take their way calmly and thoughtfully of enlightening their people as to the shameful surrender of truth and principle made by their church in violation of her own constitution, and when the time for final action shall have come, they will leave the fool's cap to be donned by such wise-heads as Mr Robertson of Rayne, and all other descendants of old Mr Pliable, whose posterity seems to be pretty numerous within the Free Church of the present day and who, according to the example set by their old ancestor always struggle out of every difficulty on the side nearest their own home."

At the Inverness Convention in June 1892 he had spoken of being brought to the verge of another Disruption. Now separation seems to be altogether out of sight, at least for the time being. They must not push the technical aspect of the protest (whatever this means), since it could only result in separation.

Finally, when the 1893 Assembly, at the conclusion of the debate in which Mr MacAskill spoke the above words, declared that even these "formal declarations" as he is pleased to term them were illegal, why did he not protest against their removal as Mr Macfarlane had the courage to do? If it were indeed true that these formal declarations remained in place to prevent the Act from being imposed on them, or "their being compelled to administer the same", was not a protest in order against this action of the removal of the protests when they lost what they claimed as a right to protect their conscientious scruples.

The whole of these statements point to the Constitutional Party by now having become merely a Party of dissent, not of protest. The historical development of this movement can be traced in the course of the intervening year.

My theory is as follows, and I think I have sufficient evidence to support it.

1. In 1892, Mr MacAskill fully intended to separate in 1894. This is the time when the Declaratory Act would become law. At this point he would leave the fool's cap on those who were weak-kneed enough not to take such a step like Mr Robertson.

2. At the June convention there was a party who were not for accepting the decision of the Convention as final till time had been given for reconsideration, possibly because they wished to wait for legal opinions on the property issue.

3. Mr MacAskill soon realised that the 1893 Assembly would not tolerate the protest as the 1892 Assembly had done. Hence, even if he meant to make a stand in 1894, he would not be able to do so if the protesting stance were not modified.

4. The legal opinions taken from both England and Scotland were not favourable. It would be difficult to make a case "stick" in the civil law courts, were the Constitutional Party to build that case on the changes made by the Declaratory Act alone. It would be

preferable to wait till the proposed union took place between the United Presbyterian Church and the Free Church. Then it would be evident that the Free Church had surrendered the Establishment principle since the United Presbyterian Church had long since rejected it, and a united church would not be able to make Establishment a matter of principle. The Free Church majority under Dr Rainy, simply by joining, would compromise their stance.

5. Mr MacAskill at first opposed the move to wait till 1900. When he realised the tide was running so strongly against him, he reluctantly fell in line.

In the next chapter I will examine these steps in order.

PART 6: THE PRESENT FREE CHURCH

CHAPTER 2

"THE SIDE NEAREST THEIR OWN HOME"

In the letter written to "The Scotsman" in August 1892, Mr MacAskill declared his intention to abide firmly by his protest against the action of the Assembly in passing the Declaratory Act "come wind, come weather." He said that they and others who would not go beyond a dissent against the Declaratory Act were like Pliable of "The Pilgrim's Progress" who got out of the Slough of Despond on the side nearest his own home. Sadly, this was to be the situation of Mr MacAskill, himself, before the year was out.

The correspondent of "The Northern Chronicle" thought that there were three parties at the June meeting at Inverness, 1892. The most extreme was represented by Mr Cameron, Back, Lewis, who, it was said, advised not paying a penny more into the Sustentation Fund. (Mr Cameron corrected this in a letter the next week. He said what he had really said was that some had advised this. At the same time, he freely admitted that he had returned from Inverness "profoundly dissatisfied with the action there taken").

Mr MacAskill's party won the immediate battle. He said in the course of his speech that he had lost all hope of the Free Church coming back to her old moorings. Nevertheless, for the time being they should fight on under cover of their protest and resolutions.

The party at the opposite extreme from Mr Cameron seems to have won the long-term battle at the Conference. It may well have been with their stance Mr Cameron was most dissatisfied. They agreed that the Conference issue a statement of their views. Nevertheless, the decision to fight under cover of their protest and resolution could be a temporary one. At the end of the various resolutions of the Conference was a relatively small resolution that could yet throw the whole stance of the Constitutional Party into the melting pot again. It ran as follows: "It is desirable that a small committee be appointed to revise the above statement, (the statement which was to be submitted to the presbyteries); and to consult with and endeavour to obtain the concurrence of brethren in other parts of the country who sympathise with us, before issuing it in the name of the Conference."

Is it any wonder Mr Cameron was profoundly dissatisfied. Doubtless, Mr Cameron looked for more decisive action at the Conference, itself. The whole statement issuing from the Conference made it clear that the response of the Party to the Declaratory Act, including the protest, could be subject to revision. If the line advocated by Mr MacAskill were followed, the protests would be entered in the Presbytery books saying that "the Act shall not be binding upon us, nor those who may now or hereafter adhere to us." If the committee appointed by the Conference decided to revise the statement, would this mean that members of the Constitutional Party might have to return to their Presbyteries at a later date with an apology saying that the line they had taken previously had been too severe, and now a much more accommodating approach had been decided on?

The disagreement within the Constitutional Party came out at the next meeting of the Constitutional Party on September 5th. The meeting was called "to assert the position they took up as regards the Declaratory Act at last General Assembly." Mention has already been made of the notice taken of this meeting in "The Northern Chronicle", and the contrast drawn between the section of the meeting and Mr Macfarlane's action in Skye. The account of the meeting given in "The Scottish Highlander," September 5th issue, is as follows;

> "The Rev. Mr MacAskill, Dingwall, presided. The proceedings, which were held in private, lasted for over two hours. A long discussion took place over a proposal to send deputations to all the Northern Presbyteries and congregations, with the object of enlisting the sympathy of the ministers in the movement, and acquainting the members and adherents of the causes which have led to the present crisis in the Church. The proposal was strongly supported by the chairman, but the other ministers and elders présent thought it would be better, in the first instance, to circulate literature bearing on the subject among the people of the Highlands and Islands. It was accordingly resolved to publish 5,000 copies of the Declaratory Act in Gaelic, together with an explanatory statement of the same, and the resolution and statement of the conclusions come to at the Conference at Inverness and Glasgow. It was resolved to meet again on the 31st October to report proceedings."

This meeting has echoes of the meeting at the time of the rebellion of Absalom when Ahithophel and Hushai gave their counsel. Ahithophel wished to pursue David directly, knowing that in the first flush of rebellion, the tide of the peoples' feeling needed an on-going momentum to ensure success. Hushai counselled caution and consolidation. Mr MacAskill was in the role of Ahithophel in a considerably better cause than the success of a rebellion. He wished the momentum of the movement to resist submission to the Declaratory Act to be maintained by living men making live and rousing speeches to individual congregations. This is perfectly in accordance with my view that Mr MacAskill meant to separate in 1894. The 5,000 copies of the Act in Gaelic would go down like a stone. (The correspondent of "The Ross-shire Journal" of Feb. 14th, 1893, calls it "trifling with a momentous question and playing into the hands of the enemy"). It was not instruction the people needed at that point but someone to point the way forward. After a cursory glance, these documents would soon find their way to the waste-paper basket.

It would seem that there was an intention to send out deputies after the 5,000 copies had been distributed, but by the next October 31st meeting, even the initial step of distributing the copies had not been taken. Indeed, absolutely nothing had been done since the last meeting of the Party. Mr MacAskill was not present at this meeting and did not even send an apology.

> "It is an open secret that the Rev. Mr MacAskill and those who have hitherto acted with him, differ as to the nature of the procedure to be adopted. It seems doubtful whether the matter will proceed further than the resolutions already arrived at. In the meantime, however, it has been resolved to invite the co-operation of Mr MacAskill to the issue of the copies of the Act and

resolutions previously arranged upon, but as it is doubtful whether certain presbyteries or congregations will receive the deputies, the next course of action has been left to a future meeting."

Like Ahithophel, Mr MacAskill is washing his hands of future proceedings. The fruit of delay is already evident. Some congregations it is now known will not receive the deputies, and as time passes, these will increase, not diminish. If the leaders of the movement are finding reason for inaction at present, reasons will become even more compelling as time passes. Inertia will become a habit, and, since the iron had not been struck while it was hot, it will become quite resistant to future moulding.

On 17th January, 1893, a private meeting of ministers was held in Edinburgh. It decided to issue the following communiqué, labelled "Private and Confidential."

"In accordance with a widely expressed desire for consultation as to united action for the future maintenance of the Constitutional principles of the Free Church, a Conference of ministers agreeing generally with the statement put forth by the Conventions at Inverness and Glasgow was held at Edinburgh on Tuesday, 17th January, 1893 at 7pm. After consultation it was agreed to submit the result of this meeting to a larger meeting to be held in Inverness...." By this time, it is evident that Mr MacAskill had come back on board since his name is found fifth on the list of ministers issuing the notice.

That meeting when it did come about was a damp squib in a whole variety of ways. Only 24 ministers attended. It was held in total secrecy. No laymen, a large number of whom came to the meeting, were admitted. When after two and a half hours, Dr Winter appeared and read a statement, the meeting was immediately closed, and Mr Galbraith, Lochalsh, launched into a totally different topic, viz. the duty of ministers to oppose a Suspensory Bill. It would seem that Dr Winter, Dyke, who had been clerk at the meeting explained to the laymen that it was necessary to await the response of the next Assembly to the Resolution they had come to that day. A party, explained Dr Winter, did not leave the Church till they were forced or persecuted, and were not permitted to explain their views or to profess their convictions.

I suppose the statement of Dr Winter might be thought as a throw-away aside in comparison with the main message contained in the official statement. Often such asides can be revealing. Why did the Constitutional party want to adopt any other stance in relation to the Assembly that that they had already adopted? They had defied the Assembly. They had said they considered the Act a new law. They had been promised relief in terms of the preamble to the Act. They had been promised that the Act would not be forced on them. Just to make perfectly evident what their stance was, they had protested after the Act had passed that they would not be subject to it. Having made perfectly clear what they represented, there was no need to give any further explanation. The ball was firmly in the Assembly's court. It was the Assembly who had promised relief. Let them now deliver it.

It seems immeasurably to weaken their position that they should adopt any other stance than they have adopted. That they did do so, and what the effect was on Dr Rainy at the next Assembly can be seen after the statement itself has been considered.

The resolution to which they were to seek the Assembly's response is as follows:

> "This meeting adheres to the position, with regard to the Declaratory Act, taken up by the convention of ministers and other office-bearers of the Free Church held at Inverness and Glasgow. This meeting therefore holds that the view given by the aforesaid Act as to the profession which is to be held consistent with the obligations laid on ministers, elders and probationers of the Free Church, cannot be harmonised with a bona fide subscription of the present formula. The validity of this position is evidenced by the proposals that are being made to change the Formula so as to adapt it to the Declaratory Act. It is confirmed by the suggestion embodied in these proposals, that the Assembly should make a declaration in the way of preamble to a new Formula, that persons signing it 'are entitled to have to do so in view of that Declaratory Act.' It being thus generally acknowledged that acceptance of the statements of the Declaratory Act cannot be reconciled with the statements regulating the profession of adherence to the doctrine, worship and government of the Church - that is with the present Formula - it appears to this meeting to be the duty of those who hold the Constitutional principles of the Free Church in the meantime to continue their protest with reference to the aforesaid Act, as being not truly declaratory, and having therefore no legal place in the Statute Book of the Free Church, and to direct their efforts towards securing, by every competent means, that this view of the Act may be given effect to."

Mr MacAskill took no official part in this meeting. Dr Aird chaired it, Dr Balfour offered up a prayer and Dr Winter acted as clerk. Dr Balfour explained the connection between the meeting in Edinburgh and the Inverness Conference.

Though it is not expressly said, it is likely this was the revision that was to follow the Inverness and Glasgow conventions. It gives the appearance of being more than a revision. It seems rather a new edition.

The first matter of surprise is the assertion that "the view given by the aforesaid (Declaratory Act, 1892) Act as to the profession which is to be held consistent with the obligations laid on ministers, elders and probationers of the Free Church, cannot be harmonised with a bona fide subscription of the present Formula" represents the view of those adhering to the 1892 Conference in June. I have gone through the six columns of fine print that give a minute account of this Conference in "The Northern Chronicle", and fail to find even one mention of Questions and Formula. All is talk of fighting under cover of the protest. How can one determine what a "bona fide" subscription to the Formula is apart from the meaning of the wording? It makes perfectly good sense to say that the subscriber is subscribing to the "whole doctrine of the Confession approven by former General Assemblies of the Free Church". As long as the General Assemblies passed acts which were in accordance with the Confession of Faith in its totality, then without doubt, the subscriber was subscribing to the whole doctrine of the Confession. If and when the Assembly passed acts which modified the Confession of Faith - and the whole Constitutional Party were in agreement that the Declaratory Act, 1892 did this - the whole doctrine approven was less than the Confession in its totality. The June, 1892 Conference, it would seem, had admitted this to be the case, and realised that the only real defence was not to seek to enlighten the majority but to refuse to implement what was now law in the Church. It is equally clear that a man like Mr Macfarlane who was present did not take that meaning out of the statement. So far as he was concerned, the only reason there had not been a full abdication of truth was that the Declaratory Act was under appeal to the court of heaven, and the General Assembly, both by its explicit declaration that relief was being sought only for some and by its action in receiving the protest after the Act was passed, had acceded to this appeal. In making their own interpretation of the resolution of June, 1892, this meeting was splitting the Constitutional party apart, and saying to such as were of Mr Macfarlane's persuasion, "We will no longer provide an umbrella under which you can shelter. You must come over to the side of those who hold that the fact of the Questions and Formula being unchanged gives the only convincing basis for saying that the Free Church has not abandoned its moorings if you are to continue with us."

After all, did the fact of the Formula being unchanged give the Constitutional Party protection?

On the merits of the case ,as above stated, it did not. Besides, the above statement contains an inherent improbability. Who is to be judge of what a "bona fide" subscription of the formula is? Those to whom the Constitutional Party henceforth has a mission "towards securing, by every competent means, that this view of the Act may be given effect to" i.e. that the Declaratory Act is unlawful, are the four fifths of the Free Church who voted for the Declaratory Act in the first place in 1891. These cheered Dr Rainy to the echo in 1893 when he dared the minority to oppress the majority by challenging them whether they were subscribing the questions "in view of the Declaratory Act." These did not surely think that the Declaratory Act was inconsistent with the present Formula. Yet the statement says that it was generally acknowledged that the statements of the Declaratory Act could not be reconciled with the Formula. "Generally acknowledged" by whom?   It is with the state of understanding in the Church at large they have to deal.   There it was not generally acknowledged that the Act was inconsistent with the terms of the Formula.   Many who were already signing the Formula with the liberty granted by the Declaratory Act were declaring openly they saw no difficulty.   Dr Rainy did not acknowledge there to be a difficulty, and the vast majority of the Assembly did not think there was any barrier to the operation of the Act either.   Yet it is insisted upon that it must be generally acknowledged that the Act was not binding because a. the Formula was to be adapted to bring it into line with the Declaratory Act, and b. persons signing the Formula were to be allowed to do so, "in view of the Declaratory Act."

Is it seriously suggested that the majority did not know what they were up to; that all the time that they were thinking that the Act was lawful, it was really unlawful, and that they were showing this by passing an Act that men could take their vows "in view of the Declaratory Act"; that all that was needed was to undertake a mission to enlighten them to their true position, and all would be well?

So far as the question of the Act being unlawful is concerned, it may have been unlawful in relation to the Constitutional Party's view of the constitution of the Church, but it was perfectly lawful so far as the law of the land was concerned.   It is here that Professor Cameron's statement quoted at the beginning of this book must be challenged.   He says that the Declaratory Act was "ultra vires" of the General Assembly.   Of course it was in the understanding of that constitution as the Constitutional Party construed it.   It was not "ultra vires" in relation to the construction that the main body of the

Church were entitled to put on the constitution. The House of Lords case proved this. They did not order the United Free Church to take the Declaratory Act from their Statute Book, simply because they knew that being a voluntary organisiation she could construe her constitution in any way she wished. The House of Lords might judge that she erred. This made no difference to her ability to pass laws in accordance with her own view of her rights, and enforce obedience from the moment these laws were passed. It is likewise meaningless, and in no way helps his case for Professor Cameron to say that the 1894 Act showed that the Declaratory Act, 1892, was merely declaratory. This simply beggs the question, declaratory of what? It was not declaratory of the Constitutional Party's view of the constitution but declaratory of the view of those bent on making "the substance of the reformed faith contained in the Confession" the measure of the constitution. The Free Church is not restricted by statute in defining its constitution, and interpreting it. The majority interpreted the constitution as allowing them to pass such an Act as the Declaratory Act, and allowing office-bearers to find refuge in the Formula as it stood, and there is nothing the minority could do about it. Certainly, any aggressive putsch to convince the majority that they did not know their own mind was doomed from the start.

The second leg of the protection claimed stems from the fact the Assembly was going to put into the preamble to a new Formula that persons signing it are entitled to do so in view of the Declaratory Act. This was to be the Declaratory Act, 1894. This, it was considered, showed that the Act was unlawful.

This Act was to be brought in in parallel with the changes in the Questions and Formula. Exactly the opposite argument could be drawn from the fact that the Act was, in fact, still passed in 1894 from that drawn by the Constitutional Party. If the change in the

Formula was aimed at bringing the (1892) Declaratory Act into operation, and the Declaratory Act, 1894, saying that therefore men could take their vows "in view of the Declaratory Act" was the explicit admission of this changed state of affairs, as the changing of the Questions and Formula was the implicit admission, one would expect that when the Formula was not, in fact, changed the Act would be withdrawn. That did not happen. Men were invited to avail themselves of the Declaratory Act. The passing of the (1894) Act, contrary to the view expreed above as to its implication, sheds a kind of reverse light on the real state of matters vis-a-vis the Questions and Formula. That Act could only be valid if it were indeed possible to avail one's self of the Act under the present, unchanged, Questions and Formula.

The whole question of whether the Declaratory Act was unlawful is really a red herring so far as the immediate duty of the Constitutional Party is concerned. After 1900, the Act was considered by them to be unlawful so far as the constitution was concerned, and this is why the remaining Constitutionalists separated. They did not go into the union claiming that the unlawfulness of the Act gave protection from the Act. The question at that time was whether they would be required to administer the Act. Because they thought they would be so required they separated. The very same question is the relevant one now. (As mentioned already, the worthies who came out at the Disruption considered the Patronage Act "null and void", and yet they separated because they knew that it was not their own private views that mattered but the operation of the Act by the civil courts). Would the Constitutional Party office-bearers be required to administer the Declaratory Act when the 1894 Act had been passed? The full text of the Declaratory Act of 1894 is as follows;

"Whereas the Declaratory Act, 1892, was passed to remove difficulties and scruples which have been felt by some in reference to the Declaration of Belief required from persons who receive licence or are admitted to office in this Church, the Assembly hereby declare that the statements of doctrine contained in the said Act are not thereby imposed upon any of the Church's office-bearers as part of the Standards of the Church, but that those who are licensed or ordained to office in this Church in answering the questions and subscribing the Formula, are entitled to do so in view of the said Declaratory Act."

The claim of the Constitutional Party was that the Standards, (basically the Confession of Faith), and the bond of union, or constitution, which bound each office-bearer to one another by his vows, is the same. All subscribe individually and collectively to the Confession of Faith. The weakness of the Constitutional stance is that they do not ask if that is the understanding of the majority. It is evident from the wording of the 1894 Act that the framers of the Act do not think that the Standards and the constitution are one and the same thing. In one and the same breath, it is said the Declaratory Act is not imposed as part of the standards of the Church, and at the same time that men may avail themselves of it. The bond of association or constitution must be wider than the Standards, (Confession of Faith). If this is not so, why introduce a special Act to safeguard the rights of those who would not submit to the Declaratory Act, though they are perfectly happy to subscribe to the Confession of Faith in its entirety, and at the same time publicly to proclaim that those who wished to gain protection from the Act could legally do so? The basis on which such an Act could be passed is revealed in the pleadings of their lawyers in 1904. The constitution as defined by the United Free Church is wider than the Confession of Faith. It regards as sacrosanct only the headship of Christ and the primacy of Scripture, deriving these from the Claim, Declaration and Protest of 1842. So wide and loose is the constitution as viewed by the majority that their Counsel had great difficulty in replying to the question put by the Lord Chancellor whether the Reformed Church might not accept the whole doctrine of the Church of Rome the very day after they had adopted the Westminster Confession of Faith! That is why they could feel perfectly at ease in passing such an Act as the 1894 Declaratory Act. Their view of the constitution is much wider than the Standards, and hence there is no contradiction from their side in saying that an Act may be passed which relieves the Free Church of strict adherance to the Standards. The argument that lies at the heart of the above statement of the Constitutional Party is a fallacy. It is not the case that the majority "generally acknowledge" that the Act is unlawful. The passage of the Act which says that office-bearers may take their vows "in view of the Declaratory Act", so far from showing that the Declaratory Act is unlawful, shows rather in a most patent way what the conviction of the majority party is on the breadth of the constitution. In staying on after the 1894 Act has been passed, and acceding to the view of the constitution given in that Act, the minority are compromising their own stance.

The only answer to the stance of the majority is the trench-warfare of protest, refusing to acknowledge the Act as binding both on themselves and on any other person in the Church. In the February 28th, 1893 statement, the Constitutional Party forsook their trenches. This is confirmed by their action in the 1893 Assembly. They decided on a kind of open warfare which was doomed to failure from the start, since they already had allowed themselves to be lured onto enemy territory, and were already colluding in what they condemned.

Dr Rainy has no need to put the second and final deliverance of the Constitutional Party under the microscope as he did the protests of the first Conference at Inverness in June, 1892, when they came up before the General Assembly in 1893. The second phase protest is simply that the Declaratory Act is not truly declaratory, a mere expression of opinion. It is not that the Act will not be binding upon them, a stance which would be accompanied with defiance. Relieved of the embarrassment of all-out opposition to the Declaratory Act, the Constitutional Party will now find a protest after the Assembly has refused to recall the Act in 1893 - a protest such as that which Mr Macfarlane presented - surplus to their requirements. The stance of the Constitutional Party is now that given by Prof. John Macleod in "Scottish Theology." The Act was unlawful given their own view of the constitution, and in that, itself, they find protection. A protest that the Act will not be binding on them can be dispensed with. The only protest now needed is expressed in the fifth Reasons of Dissent entered after the passage of the Declaratory Act in 1892:

"Because the Act now passed, ... is not and cannot be considered a Declaratory Act, but must be regarded as a new law of this Church, which alters the relations of the Church to the Confession of Faith, by substituting for the doctrines therein embodied the statement made in the Act as the future standard of orthodoxy in this Church."

If the words of Mr MacAskill in the 1892 Assembly are accepted as describing the views of the Constitutional Party as a whole at that point, when he says he would question whether men were taking their vows under the Declaratory Act, and if they said they were would bring them to the Assembly, the difference between the second phase Constitutional Party and the first phase is that at the 1892 Assembly, the Act had not only been regarded as non-declaratory, but had been admitted to be a new law, which, would immediately compromise their stance if not entirely rejected. Hence this reason of dissent had to be followed by a protest, declaring that this new law was not binding on them. That protest was quite distinct and supplementary to the statement that the Act was not Declaratory. Now there was no need of such additional protest since the Act is regarded as illegal since it clashes, it is claimed, with the Formula.

It is interesting to note about this time a letter from an unnamed Constitutionalist minister. He advocates that Dr Winter be made leader of the Constitutionalist Party. He is calm, affable and agreeable, yet modest and unassuming. (March 17th, Ross-shire Journal). Some brethren, (obviously pointing at Mr MacAskill), were so big, pompous, uncondescending and almost unapproachable "that we cannot find it any pleasure or privilege to come near them." One cannot but wonder if the irritability displayed by Mr MacAskill at this point was really due to pomposity. The symptoms may rather have been those of a brother offended who is harder to be won than a strong city. Nothing seemed to go right for him. At the February 28th Conference, he had tried to have the elders admitted to the meeting which framed the resolution and had been over-ridden. Besides, there was the delicate matter of his own conscience which he had to live with. Just two weeks before he had been saying in the Dingwall Presbytery,

> "If no change had been effected (by the Declaratory Act),
> what satisfaction had they given to their friends
> burdened with scruples? Was it not time to end this
> miserable pretence and use plain and honest speech? A
> change was intended and the change had been
> accomplished by the Declaratory Act. Men who began
> to entertain scruples about the Confession they had

voluntarily signed, and in virtue of which they held their charges, now publicly proclaimed their freedom from trammels that formerly bound them."

It is significant that these words were said in the context of a debate on the introduction of changes in the Formula. It is clear that Mr MacAskill had no illusions as to the generally accepted opinion in the Free Church, even before the new Formula was in place.

The practical fact, so far as Mr MacAskill is concerned, is that he joined with the others, and became as vocal as any of them in denouncing those who took the step of protesting after the Act had been renewed in 1893 as any other.
After all he had said against Mr Robertson's stance, and in support of all-out defiance, it would have been interesting to have been a fly on the wall the next time the two brethren met.

It is needless to emphasise that the above discussion is the very last that any minister of the gospel wishes to be involved in. It is Goliaths we wish to fight, who represent out and out enemies of the cause of God. These stir the blood, and make it a privilege to be "valiant for truth." The last situation one wishes to be involved in is one where one is drawn into debate with brethren in Christ over wire-drawn arguments. At the same time, the essence of responsibility is that one responds. Our Church is in a situation which the Free Church claims to be schismatic from the very outset. The only way to be sure one is not in a state of schism is to examine the arguments, wire-drawn as they are. Until the Free Church answer these seven questions fairly and squarely my conscience remains untroubled.

a. Had the (1843) Free Church the right to interpret her own constitution in the way she desired?

b. Was it not possible to interpret the Formula in such a way that the Declaratory Act was, indeed, being administered?

c. Did not the 1894 Act saying that men could take their vows "in view of the Declaratory Act" show that the Church encouraged ordinands to take these vows on such an understanding of the link between the Declaratory Act and the vows taken that they openly sanctioned such an understanding, thus throwing a cloak of protection over those who did so?

d. Could the Constitutional Party do anything to prevent this?

e. In the light of this, did not the removal of the right of protest in 1893 take away the last serious means of opposing the Declaratory Act?

f. Were not any who made up a Presbytery where an office-bearer took his vows under the Declaratory Act administering the Declaratory Act along with all other members of Presbytery?

g. In that case, how can anyone be charged with schism in separating from such a Church when those who make this charge separated, themselves, in 1900, not because they could not preach the whole doctrine of the Confession in the United Free Church as they did in the Free Church, but because they, too, would have to administer the Declaratory Act and found in this an adequate reason for leaving?

h. In the light of this, why did the Free Church not unite with and make common cause with the Free Presbyterian Church which had separated seven years earlier?

SECTION 6: THE PRESENT FREE CHURCH

CHAPTER 3

"I STAYED AND LINGERED LONG."

The action of the Constitutional Party in 1892 and on into 1893 noted in the previous chapter does seem to demand explanation. The popular support was there directly after the 1892 Assembly. Reports in influential papers like "The Glasgow Herald" and in "The Scotsman" after the June 1892 Convention spoke with a measure of approval of the movement. The Glasgow Herald said that the minority "which is poor in purse and by no means skilled in Biblical Criticism has decidedly the best of the argument." Why then first the delay, and then after many months the proclamation of a statement quite at variance with the spirit of the June, 1892, Convention?

A possible answer is hinted at from a variety of sources. A pamphlet issued by Rev Mr Macdonald, Applecross, compares unfavourably the steps taken by the Constitutionalists and the break made by the Disruption Church.

"These fathers, however, proved the reality of their convictions by the course they adopted, and surely those who believe that the Free Church has become so corrupt that she is more than useless should do likewise. Those fathers, however, proved the reality of their convictions by the course they adopted, and if we believe that the Free Church has become so corrupt that she is worse than useless, our duty clearly is to follow their noble example. This course is delayed until the minority, i.e. the Constitutionalists, make sure of all the Free Church property.   Alas, how are the mighty fallen?" ("The Declaratory Act and a Second Disruption", p. 11).

In 1893, Allan Mackenzie, one of the students who joined the Free Presbyterian Church is more explicit.   At a meeting held on 30 June, 1893, Mr Mackenzie says,

"as to the leaders of the Constitutional Party, of whom they wished to speak with every respect, they, (the F.P. Church), repudiated the charge that they insinuated that these leaders were now going after the loaves and fishes, but they must look at the facts.   What were the facts? These leaders took the opinion of counsel twice.   They took that opinion last winter, consulting the most eminent counsel in England as well as Scotland, to see about the property, because they had no right to consult counsel upon any other point."

Perhaps these references might not be worth mentioning - they were, after all, both opponents of the post-1893 Constitutional Party - if their views were not supported by the counsel for the Free Church in the trial of 1904. Mr Johnson says in reference to the modifying effect of the Declaratory Act of 1894 upon the original Declaratory Act of 1892,

> "I do not say that goes the whole length, but it goes some way at any rate in modifying the effect of the Declaratory Act. Now it is held up against us, 'Why do you not secede then?' My Lords, I do not admit that there is a duty of secession in a case of that sort. There is a duty of resistance and of taking action when the first opportunity comes, and we have done so. We have certainly resisted, and when it comes to touch property, then is our opportunity, and our only and first opportunity to effectively resist. It now does come to property, when, following that out, they commence in 1896, their union campaign. That also is resisted, and every step in that is contested by the minority I represent."

This statement by Mr Johnson raises a number of questions, but for the time being it is sufficient to note that there is a frank acknowledgement that the reason for waiting to 1900 before separation had to do with the greater likelihood of gaining the property at that date.

The reasoning behind this was as follows. Quite apart from reducing the adherence to the Confession of Faith to no more than the substance of the Reformed faith, there were two main reasons why the Constitutional Party believed that the Declaratory Act changed the Free Church constitution. One had to do with certain heads of doctrine, and is referred to in the first reason of dissent in 1892.

The second reason was

"Because under the head which refers to intolerant and persecuting principles, which is to take the place of the present preamble to the Formula, all reference to the duties of nations and their rulers to true religion and the Church of Christ, as therein set forth, is wholly omitted, whereby the testimony of this Church to that important doctrine is dropped, while the allusions to the teaching of the Confession is so introduced, as to imply that the doctrine is intolerant and persecuting; and thus, both directly and by implication, this distinctive doctrine of the Free Church is set aside, and full liberty is given to such as hold and teach voluntary principles to subscribe the Confession."

This latter issue was called the Establishment principle. The terms in which the Declaratory Act referred to this point are as follows,

"That this Church disclaims intolerant or persecuting principles, and does not consider her office-bearers, in subscribing the Confession, committed to any principles inconsistent with liberty of conscience and the right of private judgement."

It was one thing to be persuaded, themselves, as they clearly were from the Reason of Dissent, that this clause - vague and ambiguous as it is - jettisoned the Establishment principle. It was another to prove before a civil court of law that it did.

By 1904, the great majority of the Free Church had joined with the United Presbyterian Church. This church, beyond question, opposed the Establishment principle. Hence, there could be no doubt that a church that combined both United Presbyterian and Free Churches could not impose adherence to this doctrine as an essential item of belief. It would be more easy, at that point, to show that the Establishment doctrine had ceased to operate.

The case as presented to the House of Lords was that the Declaratory Act had, indeed, altered the relation of the Free Church to the Standards, both in relation to the doctrines of the Confession and the Establishment Principle. Nevertheless, the great proof that the United Free Church did not have the same witness as the Free Church rested on the simple fact of union to a body professing a contrary view on the Establishment Principle. As the matter turned out, five out of seven of the judges did agree that the Establishment principle was a fundamental principle of the Free Church from its commencement. Hence they found for the minority on this side of the argument, since the U.F. Church clearly could not regard the Establishment Principle as other than an open question. Three out of seven found for the minority on the changes they claimed had been introduced in the Declaratory Act. Two of the judges said they would not give an opinion on the matter since the change in the relation to the Establishment principle was enough to enable them to find in the favour of the minority. Had either of them favoured the minority on this point, it would have been enough win the case simply on the basis of the changes brought in by the Declaratory Act, without reference to the Establishment principle.

Why does Mr Johnson say that it comes to property in 1900? That is not strictly correct. The moment there is an admission that the doctrinal standards of a church have been changed it comes to property. The civil courts will pass judgement on which side represents the true and original constitution of the church concerned. The Free Presbyterian Church could have gone to the civil courts in 1893 and claimed that the Declaratory Act had introduced radical changes to the constitution of the Free Church and that they had a right to claim the property. What Mr Johnson is really saying is that there would have been a much greater likelihood of gaining the property by means of a separation in 1900 than if separation had taken place in 1893 or 1894, since by that time, by virtue of the the accomplishment of the union, it would have become perfectly clear the Free Church had compromised her stance on Establishment.

If this, indeed, was the reason for the delay, for the secret meetings, and for the seeming change in the view of the leaders of the Constitutionalists as to the immediate gravity of the crisis in 1892 when they did eventually issue their statement, may be a matter of opinion. What is not a matter of opinion is that the Constitutional Party seemed in 1892 to be set on separation. The eventual statement issued in February, 1893, prior to the Assembly would seem to be so worded that they would be able to sail past the next danger point in 1894, when the Declaratory Act would, without any dubiety, be brought into operation, and no crisis would be provoked. If they could say they were protected in 1894 from complicity in the Act because the Questions and Formula had not been changed, they could then feel free to wait on till the union between the U.P. Church and the Free Church took place, and then raise a law case after separation.

Of course Mr MacAskill and his colleagues said they would never administer the Declaratory Act, and that, it would seem, satisfied their followers. If you mean that the words, "Declaratory Act" did not enter into ordinations after 1894, and you took the same meaning from the Formula which the Constitutional Party did, then they did not administer the Act. If you mean that the Declaratory Act was on the statute-book, that the Church by the Act of 1894 made it perfectly plain that it was there to be used, and that they made equally plain how it could be used, i.e. by taking a certain meaning from the Questions and Formula, then they were administering the Declaratory Act. The question is, which meaning was the really operative one. Without doubt, it was the second. The Constitutional Party was administering the Declaratory Act all along, and Mr MacAskill, by his statements in 1892 makes plain that he knew perfectly well that this would be the case.

My concern in raising this issue at present does not have to do with the Free Church directly. It has to do with the relationship that developed over the period 1892-93 between Mr Macfarlane and the main part of the Constitutional Party. The viewpoint of the students in 1892 was that the protest of 1892 should have led to separation. After they united with Mr Macfarlane and Mr Macdonald to form the Free Presbyterian Church, they carried this view into the Free Presbyterian Church though the view could not to be applied to the 1892 protest - since separation did not take place then - but rather to the 1893 protest. If one says that the protest of 1892 should have led to separation as the students did, then both Mr MacAskill and Mr Macfarlane were at fault. Both adhered to the protest, both did not separate, both proclaimed their right to remain in the Free Church under protest. Only when one admits the right of the protester to claim protection under protest, can one can go on to trace the descent of the main part of the Constitutional Party into a party of dissent, and see where the real difference between Mr MacAskill and Mr Macfarlane lay in the Assembly of 1893. Mr Macfarlane, still claimed the right of the protest of 1892 to protect his conscience, (what he, himself, thought of as an essential accompaniment to his appeal to the Court of heaven, according to his Kishorn lecture), and now protested against the removal of that right. Mr MacAskill simply dissented. The one was forced into separation, while the other was able to continue in the Free Church.

There are other reasons why the Constitutional Party thought they were untouched by the Declaratory Act, 1893-1900. Such were arguments arising from the fact that the commission issued to those who attended Assemblies called on them to pass laws in accordance with "the Word of God, the Confession of Faith, and the constitution of this Church". As already mentioned, the view that the majority had on the constitution of the church was wider than their view of the Standards. They argued in the House of Lords case, indeed, that the constitution of the Scottish Church embraced a right to change the standards, as had been done in the adoption of the Westminster Confession in the place of the old Scottish Confession at the time of the Second Reformation. Hence, while in normal circumstances judgement was passed at General Assemblies in accordance with the Westminster Confession, there could be exceptional circumstances when the particular part of the constitution was brought into play which allowed them to change the Confession of Faith, itself.

The outworking of these views would argue that it is the Free Presbyterian Church which has right to claim to be the continuing Free Church rather than the Free Church. As long as the Free Presbyterian Church holds to the view that the true breach between Mr Macfarlane and the Constitutional party is to be seen in that he presented a protest and separated in 1893 and the main body of the Constitutional Party did not, such arguments as I have set out above are not open to them. Only when it is admitted that Mr Macfarlane agreed with the same protest as his brethren entered after the Declaratory Act was passed in 1892, agreed with the June convention in their resolve to enter their protest in the lower courts of the Church, proceeded to do so, and then protested in 1893 against the undermining of the protesting stance, can the true stance of Mr Macfarlane vis-à-vis the Constitutional Party be appreciated. Both Mr Macfarlane and the Constitutionalists began in 1892 with the stance that a protest was a *sine qua non* to preserve the conscientious stance of the Party. Throughout the year, the Constitutional Party fell back into a stance of dissent.

It will not be surprising that I feel that only when the Free Presbyterian change their view of protest and the Church comes round to a true view on the nature and the effect of a protest will the crux of the real difference between them and the continuing Free Church be clarified. Until then they will always be vulnerable to an attack by that Church on the basis of schism, and will never be able to present their case to advantage.

The Free Church will be under attack because they began with true views on the rights of private judgement and liberty of conscience, but jetissoned them after the June Conference, 1892. Mr Macfarlane alone carried through to the bitter end the logic of their earlier position. Did the Free Church sacrifice an open door to the court of heaven, such as Mr Macfarlane presents in his Kishorn address, for an open door to the law-courts?

PART 7: THE APC CASE

CHAPTER 1

"HOW GREAT A MATTER...."

The separation of the Associated Presbyterian Churches took place after the trial of two cases in the 1989 Synod. In this chapter I suggest a number of ways in which the Free Presbyterian Church may be said to have neglected to follow correct lines of procedure in consideration of these cases. In the next chapter I go on to consider the way in which an overture was dealt with by the Synod. Since the overture deals with principle, it seems to me to be of much greater importance than the details of management of the two cases.

Lord Mackay was suspended for attending a mass at the funeral of a friend in the legal profession. Rev. A. Murray was suspended for asking a Roman Catholic priest to pray at a Regional Council meeting where he, himself, was acting as chairman.

The first objection against both sentences of suspension is that the basis for the sentence on either side was not a standing law of the Church setting out the principles involved in each without entering into the merits of any particular situation. When a civil court passes sentence, the basis of condemnation is the law of the land. Where no law condemns the practice under trial, there can be no sentence.

One possible reply is that the Church has a standing law-book in the Scriptures. There is no need for any separate law-book condemning murder or adultery. The commandments do this already.

This only makes it all the more necessary that the particular practice be one that is clearly condemned by Scripture before any process is entered upon. "It has been established by long practice that no judicial process of a serious kind can be carried out against a minister or a probationer, except by the use of what is called a Libel ..... The first or major proposition, sets forth the nature of the alleged offence, declares its contrariety to the Word of God and the laws of the Church, and indicates the kind of consequences which ought to follow from it." (p.88). In the case of Mr Murray, since there were no ready-made laws of the Church relevant to the claimed offence, so the part referring to such laws is irrelevant. The Word of God must be the sole witness. The one argument I remember being urged with force was that none of the Reformers would have asked a member of the Church of Rome to pray. Even that is questionable, since Samuel Rutherford says, "The Church of Rome hath something of the life and being of a Church, howbeit she be not a whole Church.....2. Because the word of God and so the contract of Marriage is professed among them, and so there is an external active calling there, and the word of the covenant sounding amongst them, and a passive calling also, because many secretly believe and obey. 3. Many fundamental truths are taught that may beget faith, and so there are true and valid pastoral acts in that Church." ("Paul's Presbytery." ch. 10) The one essential point was to determine what the Scriptures said about the whole circumstances of the case Mr Murray was involved in. That was never forthcoming.

A further reason why it was important that Scripture was made the rule of judgement is that both fell into the category of what the Confession of Faith calls "cases of conscience." (XXXI.III). What marks cases of conscience is that Scriptural evidence may be presented on both sides of the argument. The strands of Scripture evidence must be teased out. The relative importance given to each strand of evidence must be weighed. Decrees and determinations which resolve such cases of conscience will be complex.

In the case of Lord Mackay who attended a mass without partaking in the ceremony, the principal Scriptural evidence brought against his action was the command to flee from idolatry, (1 Cor. 10;14). The mass being an idolatrous rite according to Protestant doctrine he should have been nowhere near it. This immediately begs the question whether one is actually involved in idolatry at all simply by being present when the mass is performed. I have been, myself, and I was not conscious merely as an observer that I was partaker in an idolatrous rite. If Scriptural sanction is sought for this point of view, it can be found in the fact that the three children in Babylon did not think their faithfulness to God's will was in any way compromised by being in the presence of the idol in the plain of Dura. Compromise was involved only when they knelt. Hence a person might be in the presence of the performance of a mass, and sin only be involved when they actively entered into the service.

Suffice it to say that there were sufficient strands of evidence on either side to make it evident that a careful weighing of the evidence was in order.

The same was true in Mr Murray's case. What would Scripture have to say about asking a Church of England clergyman of the "high" section of that church to pray. They have the same doctrinal beliefs as the Romanists with the exception that they have the monarch as the head of the Church in place of the Pope. If such a clergyman had been asked to pray, would similar action have been taken? If Roman Catholic baptism is allowed, then surely the prayer that forms an essential part of that rite is condoned. What does Scripture have to say about this? On a wider sphere, the Church lost direct control of social issues and educational issues when the parochial system dissolved. May it not claim a right to serve on such committees in order to have an influence on such issues, and in the process, may not several practices in which the Free Presbyterian Church would not otherwise be involved be condoned? What is the Scriptural rule to guide us? In no sense was the committee meeting constituted by the initial prayer, as a church court would have been. In this case, the significance of prayer at the beginning was no more than if one were to ask a Roman Catholic to ask a blessing on food.

The whole emphasis of the Reformed Church, as I have sought to point out in the preceding pages, has been to give as full liberty to the conscience of the individual as possible. Consider such a statement as that of George Gillespie, one of the commissioners to the Westminster Assembly.

> "Presbyterial power doth not lord it over men's consciences, but admitteth, (yea commendeth), the searching of the Scriptures, whether those things which it holds forth be not so, and doth not press men's consciences with *sic volo, sic iubeo,* ('thus I wish, thus I command'), but desireth that they may do in faith what they do."

Was the Free Presbyterian Church conscious of the right of private judgement, and the tenderness with which cases of conscience should be dealt? Was the Free Presbyterian Church conscious of the rights of conscientious minorities? Was it ready to allow divers views in the Church, perhaps over long periods till clear light on duty was obtained? Was it consciously ready to allow divergent practices, and to protect these under the umbrella of the church, without forcing either absolute and blind obedience on another or explicit faith where only one side of an Scriptural argument was given prominence at the exception of another?

Even had a resolution been come to which the majority in all conscience believed to represent Scripture truth, it is not the reformed practice to expel those who cannot abide by these views unless it is clearly evident that only pretended liberty is claimed. The actions of the Synod gave the suspicion that they were not acting according to clearly defined rules laid out in the Confession of Faith governing the dealing with private judgement. It was in the light of this rejection of these vital sections of the Confession rather than in the light of the actual treatment of the particular cases before the Synod that separation took place.

The overture brought out the Confessional teaching, and it is to this I will turn in the next chapter.

PART 7; THE APC CASE

CHAPTER 2;

THE TEXT OF THE OVERTURE

The overture presented to the 1989 Synod was largely, if not wholly, the work of Rev. Alex. Murray. It was in these terms.

"It is overtured by the undersigned members of the Synod of the Free Presbyterian Church of Scotland to the ensuing Synod that

1. Whereas the Scripture allows a sure place within the Christian Church to both the weak and the strong, each with his right of private judgement in matters relating to the application of his Christian faith to daily living, although in such application one may differ from the other, as in Romans 14 and especially verse 3, 'Let not him that eateth despise him that eateth not; and let not him that eateth not judge him that eateth; for God hath received him.'

2. And whereas, a.) the Westminster Confession in Chapter XX Section II stating that 'God alone is Lord of the Conscience', b.) the Larger Catechism 105 stating that it is a sin against in breach of the First Commandment to make 'men the lords of our faith and conscience', and c.) the Manual of Practice at p.66 stating 'that the Free Presbyterian Church maintains most emphatically that no authority of the Synod has any absolute rule over the

consciences of believers,' preserve and enjoin the duty of private judgement;

3. And whereas the Roman Catholic Church, on the other hand, erroneously teaches in terms of the Council of Florence (1439 A.D.) that this power and authority belongs *iure divino* to the Pope, viz. ' the primacy or supremacy over the whole world; that he is the successor of St. Peter, the Prince of the apostles, the true vicar of Christ, the head of the whole church, and the father and teacher of all Christians; and that in St. Peter full power was given to him by our Lord Jesus Christ of feeding, ruling and governing the universal church';

4. The Synod, believing that these important principles enshrined in the Scriptures and constitution of this Church are vital to the faithful life and witness of this Church, and the people within its communion,

DECLARES that the maintenance of due order within this denomination does not require from its office-bearers and members a rigid uniformity of practice, an implicit faith and an absolute and blind obedience, and further,
DECLARES that all courts of this Church shall have regard to this declaration of Synod in all cases before them relating to the exercise of discipline and the granting of Church privileges,

Or that they do otherwise for this object what to their wisdom may seem best.....".

The overture illustrating the use of the open door.

In underlining private judgement, section 2 of the overture deals with the way Christ communicates with us by way of the open door, and the way by which we, on our side, discern his will. It is by private judgement of what the Scriptures say. (Private judgement presupposes Christian liberty, as I sought to show earlier, and is always bound by Scripture, since the judgement arrived at never represents judgement formed merely according to our own whims and fancies.)

Section 2 also deals with the additional fact that men may stand in the way of direct obedience to Christ, calling us to listen rather to what they say, and that when we submit to this, we are "making men the lords of faith and conscience."

Section 3 takes an illustration of an organisation, officially organised on the model of the vertical line of rule - the Roman Catholic Church. The Pope is "the vicar of Christ" on earth. Hence, having such powers granted to him, it is the Pope's "yea" or "nay" which determines whether a particular view will receive sanction or not in the Roman Catholic Church. Both sides in the debate - the Free Presbyterian Church and the Associated Presbyterian Churches - follow Protestant doctrine. Hence, surely both sides should be united in opposition to such interference. There is also the implied claim - which was already noted in Rev. M MacAskill's defence of the protest of 1892 - that when the courts of the Church rule with absolute sway, these courts become the equivalent of the Pope. They prevent the exercise of true liberty. The correct means of opposition to such an assertion is to emphasise the priesthood of all believers as over against the unique claims made by the hierarchy of the Church of Rome, or such powers as would exercise a like dominance.

Section 4 shows what the resulting effect will be on the Church from the adoption of such views. Where a person says it is respect for Christ's will, as that is seen in His word, (private judgement), which causes him to adopt a certain stance, the Church should not summarily condemn him. Where two people make the same claim, coming to differing views on the same subject by honest examination of Scripture, (as in Romans 14), neither side should be evicted from the Church. Each can claim direct access to the court of heaven.

The first concluding appeal to the Synod, ("The Synod...... declares that the maintenance of due order etc."), shows what the resulting effect will be. Out of deference to Christ, the head of the Church, there will be no attempt to force rigid uniformity upon two sections within the same church who respectively hold differing views on the same topic, and who each hold these views on the basis of honest examination of the Scripture evidence.

The mention of "implicit faith" and "absolute and blind obedience" is introduced to show that church courts, themselves, in framing their determinations, will have a duty to use Scripture in exactly the same way as that in which individuals within the Church use it. Church courts are subject to the court of heaven as well as the individual, and can only have claim to the obedience of the individual if and when they are channels for the voice of Christ. "Absolute and blind obedience" is obedience in matters of faith and worship to determinations which do not have their origin in Scripture. "Implicit faith" is faith required in a particular interpretation of Scripture on which a determination might be based, simply on the "say-so" of the court, without allowing the liberty for other views to be entertained. Both absolute and blind obedience and implicit faith would deny the prime right of an individual to take understanding of duty direct from Christ.

The practical result so far as the rule of the courts is concerned is two-fold. There should be no rigid uniformity forced on two groups within the Church who hold differing views on a particular topic, provided, as the Evangelical Manifesto would put it, both are clearly framing their views on Scripture. Likewise, when the final decision of the court, itself, becomes a focus for disagreement, (rather than the differeing views of two members within the Church), there should be no rigid uniformity imposed by the court in an attempt to rule out diversity of views in favour of uniformity. Claims based on the word of God that the courts are attempting to impose "absolute and blind obedience" or "implicit faith" will be respectfully examined. The permission of these differing views will be no sign of weakness. It will rather be a sign of strength, an evidence that Christ is allowed to reign freely in His Church.

The key issues of the overture are, then, the duty of private judgement, the right to claim God as lord of the conscience, liberty of conscience to oppose men's views in matters pertaining to faith and worship, the right of co-existence within the Church of members having differing views, the right to oppose implicit faith and absolute and blind obedience, and the duty of the church to allow liberty of expression within the Church to views which may differ from the accepted line.

The overture was rejected. It is needless to go over the ground already covered by which I have sought to show that the (1843) Free Church was based on such principles, and the separation of Mr Macfarlane took place on such principles. The contrary view of rigid adherence to resolutions of the Supreme Court came in with the stance of the students on the Declaratory Act. It became the firmly entrenched view of the Free Presbyterian Church. Hence, it was not surprising that the overture was rejected.

By virtue of the overture, the Associated Presbyterian Church can claim to have resurrected these basic principles.

I trust that now my Free Church brother in Skye will see the validity of the principles on which the Associated Presbyterian Churches rests, and my Free Presbyterian brother will see why I do not consider myself a prodigal.

PART 8: THE CONCLUSION

CHAPTER 1

RETURN TO THE MANSE

I must now attempt to tie all these threads together and show their relevance to the point at which I entered on this discussion, viz. the question of who the rightful owners of the Kinlochbervie manse were. Since the title deeds were in the name of the Free Presbyterian Church, and I from 1989 was not in that Church, it is perfectly understandable that questions could be raised as to my continuing occupation of the manse.

First, those who hold that the maintenance of due order does not require of office-bearers or members of the Church rigid uniformity of practice, implicit faith and absolute and blind obedience to Synod rulings, since the Synod is composed of but fallible men (1989 Overture), hold by a fundamental point of the constitution.

In registering his accord with the protest entered in 1892, Mr Macfarlane did not think that the refusal to give his implicit faith to the ruling of the Supreme Court and afford blind obedience to the Declaratory Act and the consequent lack of uniformity that this introduced into the practice of the Church disrupted the maintenance of due order. There is no inconsistency, in his view, in having a protesting minority remaining on in the Free Church refusing to give submission to the views of the majority. He adopted this stance as a means of upholding his constitutional rights, and his position under protest was itself an assertion of constitutional privileges granted by the Confession of Faith.

The "Claim, Declaration and Protest", which is a constituent part of the constitution of the Free Presbyterian Church, expresses similar views. The "Declaration" section expresses views about private judgement and the exercise of Scriptural liberty of conscience which give the Church the right to oppose ideas in the realm of faith and worship which run contrary to the the Scriptures.

The Evangelicals of the 18th century are seen to adopt a similar position. The maintenance of due order, they maintain, may still be upheld when rulings of the Supreme Court are made final but not binding. Since every man has

> "an inalienable right to judge for himself, as he will be answerable to the Lord; a right which he cannot give up to any man or society of men; because it is not merely his privilege, but his indispensable duty", "subscription and engagement to obedience and submission to the judicatories of the church is with the express limitation of its being in the Lord."

All these parties, then, Mr Macfarlane, the Disruption fathers, and the Evangelicals of the 18th century, and the framers of the Westminster Confession, not to speak of earlier illustrations of protesters taken from Reformation times would have had no difficulty in subscribing to the Overture of 1989 as expressing rights fundamental to the constitution of the Reformed Church.

On the other hand, the Moderates, and those who opposed the Disruption fathers would, in consistency with their expressed opinions, have had to oppose and reject the 1989 Overture. They would have argued that the maintenance of due order requires universal obedience, and that the expression of liberty of conscience is confined to liberty to oppose in principle, (dissent), but not in practice, (protest), rulings of the Supreme Court to which one is conscientiously opposed. The entry of this view into the Free Presbyterian Church is not to be traced from Mr Macfarlane, but from the students who joined him in 1893. These accepted without question the views of Dr Rainy to whom Mr Macfarlane was opposed. He would not admit the possibility of the right of protest against a law of the Supreme Court. From the time of the judgement in the case of Rev. Ewan Macqueen, this view has become the accepted view in the Free Presbyterian Church.

May I respectfully ask how, in the view of those who gathered to celebrate the tabling of Mr Macfarlane's protest in 1893, the constitution of the (1843) Free Church was preserved inviolate in the period 1892-93. Was it not by a continuation of the witness of the protesting minority which had been in existence since 1892, and by protesting against the withdrawal of the right of protest by a despotic majority? Between 1892 and 1893, the protesting minority supported private judgement, liberty of conscience, and opposed implicit faith and did not see the maintenance of due order impaired by the expression of these values.   In supporting Mr Macfarlane's protest, then, Free Presbyterians are supporting these issues, and yet these very values are denied in the rejection of the 1989 overture. We are entitled to repeat the question, then, "How was the constitution of the Reformed Church was upheld 1892-1893?"

I have striven for the acknowledgement of these rights since 1971. My support of the 1989 overture was the latest expression of that support. These are constitutional rights. Hence I am upholding the "Constitution and whole Standards of the Free Presbyterian Church". It logically follows, then, since *"in case any disruption or secession shall take place in said congregation the said subjects and others shall be held in trust for the sole use and behoof of, and shall belong to the section of the said congregation, whether they be the majority or minority of the same, who adhere to the said Constitution and the whole Standards and the said Protest last mentioned (the Protest contained in the Deed of Separation) in all particulars," (Title Deeds),*

I, as minister of the section of the congregation which seceded, in faithful adherence to the expression of fundamental rights contained in the Constitution and Standards of the Free Presbyterian Church as expressed in the 1989 Overture, could not be said to have been in unlawful occupation of the manse.

It also follows that since the views of 1989 are not the views of any individual alone, but the views of the Associated Presbyterian Churches, the congregation which represents that denomination may rightfully possess the manse even though no minister is resident at the present.

The property issue, so far as the well-being of the Church at large is concerned, is a side-issue, and should never have centre-stage. "After all these things do the Gentiles seek." On the other hand, the inconsistency percieved in remaining in occupation of buildings, seemingly without proper reason, makes this the most highly visible effect of the division, particularly for those who have no time or patience to enter into the debate. Hence it is needful that some defence be given.

PART 8 - THE CONCLUSION

CHAPTER 2

MODELS AND REALITY

Each of us has a model of ourselves, and we do not take kindly to having that model challenged. A person caught looking through a key-hole will feel shame, not only because another has seen them spying, but because they think, "That is not really the person I am."

In this final chapter, I wish to examine the models the various parties I have spoken of have projected, and question whether they will bear analysis.

First, what of the model of omnicompetent man. Do our researches of the present day bear out his omnicompetency to fit a rational theory to all he has found? Can the worm submit the stock exchange to a comprehensive survey, using the full power of its intellect. A report in "The Times" suggests he cannot. A Professor Edward Harrison of the University of Masschusetts reports a point that has been noted by not a few over the last period. "We do not know why natural qualities such as the strength of gravity, the speed of light, the electric charge on the electron, and so on have the values they do. Yet the slightest variation of their values would result in a barren universe without stars or light." Why it might be thought is this issue so vital?

We have been used, for instance, to the wonders that are presented in the adaptability of man to his environment. Why, for instance, does he breathe in precisely the gas he does - oxygen - which plants breathe out, and hence keep in plentiful supply? Given current wisdom, the atheist can sit easy to such a question. If you shovel in enough millions of years, then you have time for all the varieties of man to appear, one, perhaps breathing methane, one hydrogen, one ozone etc.. The unsuitable are eliminated, and the specimen that breathes oxygen which is in plentiful supply and is replenished by expiration from plants is preferred. By contrast, what is unique about the physical building-blocks of the Universe is that time is precisely what one does not have. Electrons, protons, neutrons etc. are there from the start. There is no time for adaptation and accommodation. The illustration of the apologist, Paley, is exactly true when he says that if one found a watch which was perfectly in order, one would be correct in concluding that an intelligent being had created it. Just so, all the constituent elements of the universe must be there in perfect balance from the start. Is it any wonder, then, that Professor Edward Harrison goes on to say, "There are two answers to this question. One is that a Supreme Being - God - designed the Universe in just the form needed for life. But that answer precludes further rational enquiry." In other words, man would have to accept a world, the world of the divine purpose, which his reason could not penetrate.

So far as the underlying reality that undergirds the universe is concerned, another scientist, Professor A. Brian Pippard of Cambridge University considers what is a real table. Is it the table we see, or is it the table we know is there quite apart from our seeing, or is it the table that scientists theorise about made up of atoms and electrical fields? His conclusion is that there is a fourth table, "although a scientist cannot say anything positive about the nature of the fundamental reality, beyond asserting that there must be something real underpinning the astonishing coherence of his physical world." In reality, he is saying a lot that is positive about this reality. It is singular, it is unseen, it is incomprehensible, and it clearly has a reasoning power beyond the wildest reaches of our imagination if it underpins the coherence of the physical world. That sounds very much like what the theist would call "God".

Man's own searching, then leads him to the conclusion that it is not man who is in the driving seat. It is a being unseen, incomprehensible, and one in whom we all live and move and have our being. The scientist here is at a very far remove from the scientists of last century who claimed that given time we should become gods. Another scientist, Sir Arthur S. Eddington says, "I am convinced that a just appreciation of the physical world as it is understood today carries with it a feeling of open-mindedness toward a wider significance transcending scientific measurement, which might have seemed illogical a generation ago." Professor Pippard again says, "It is tempting for the scientist, with the assurance he commands in his own realm, to dismiss religious experience as a delusion. To be sure, he has the right to parade the evidence that makes him sceptical of antiquated cosmologies such as religions are apt to carry in their train; and he is right to despise dogmas that imply a God whose grandeur does not match up to the grandeur of the universe he knows. But when we have chased out the mountebanks, there remain the saints and others of transparent integrity whose confident belief is not to be dismissed simply because it is inconvenient and unshared. We may lack the gift of belief ourselves, just as we may be tone-deaf; but it is becoming in us to envy those whose lives are radiant with a truth which is no less true for being incommunicable."

As a confession of faith, that may rank as less than convincing. It is all the more telling for that. Looking from the side of the physical universe, Professor Pippard is acknowledging that there is, in all likelihood, a side to the universe that eye does not see, nor ear hear, nor does it enter into the heart of man naturally to understand, and that there may be an open door from that region to those endowed with the ability to respond to it. That is the point to which his science has led the modern scientist.

Much of unbelieving Higher Criticism came from the "spill-over" into the world of Biblical Criticism from the confidence in man's powers that was evident in the secular world. Miracles were thought of by many researchers to be unbelievable, and only came into the gospel record as a testimony to the credulity of the on-lookers. Likewise, it was thought that to say too deprecatory things about man as Paul does in Romans did not match up to reality. We should be cured of that notion now after seeing what civilised man can do to his fellow in recent wars. A hundred years on from the Declaratory Act which allowed freedom from Confessional bonds in the Free Church, and hence freedom to speculate freely on who the real Jesus was beyond the gospel records, confusion remains. Dr Rainy spoke in the course of the Declaratory Act debate on the need to set the most brilliant minds free to pursue the truth for the benefit of all. The model is of brilliance finding for the benefit of all the Holy Grail of truth, and putting us all into their eternal debt by bringing it back and setting it at the feet of the lowliest in the land.

My aim is simply to ask, did all the researches find the truth? In 1893 there were those who saw how flawed the model was. Nevertheless, it is of interest to see how there has been such a swing away from these views in sections of those who were themselves brought up in the school of liberal theological study. Needless to say, the neo-orthodox views of Karl Barth are not the views of the churches which subscribe wholly to the Westminster Confession of Faith. Nevertheless, Karl Barth, though educated as a liberal, saw that the Bible claimed to criticise men, even, perhaps particularly, the wise and prudent. "He takes the wise in their own craftiness." How, then, can a scientific study of the Scriptures by men who are themselves the subject to the Bible's criticism end in finding the truth? There must be submission to that word before we know the truth of it. There is no open door from man to God. Scripture brings an open door from God to man. That door we can only avail ourselves of when first by faith we receive God's revelation. "Ye shall know the truth, and the truth shall set you free."

So far as the Free Presbyterian Church is concerned, I am more on home ground. This Church claims to continue on the Church of the Reformation. The vows tie office-bearers to the Westminster Confession of Faith. The image is of a pure Church which can criticise institutions and Government without fear because it carries forward the bed-rock principles of the Word of God, and applies these without fear or favour.

Considering that my whole life was spent in the Free Presbyterian Church until 1989, it will not be surprising that I subscribe to the fundamentals of what that Church holds by. I gladly owe my debt to many in that church, and separation has not broken gospel bonds. The question I confine myself to at present is, does the model represent the reality?

The model is of a whiter than white Church. There is a petition in prayer I was used to hearing I was used to hearing, and which will be immediately recognised by anyone brought up in the Church, "May we never bring a spot upon thy Cause." That is a worthy petition. Nevertheless, the impression conveyed was that the Cause, it would seem, is for ever unsullied. We are the ones who are sullied and may defile the cause. When I brought up the question of the possibility of error in both fact and interpretation of the protest of 1893, and the question of unjustified separations on the basis of that interpretation, I was told to go back to my "ordinary and vital duties." My ordinary and vital duties take to do with directing individuals to "repentance toward God and faith in Jesus Christ." They do not take to do with directing the Church to repentance. Yet the very Confession of Faith which the Church gloried in declared that "All Synods or councils .... may err, and many have erred." The vows by which I was bound, and which the Church equally gloried in, instructed me to oppose error and schism, "notwithstanding of whatsoever trouble and persecution arose." How can the Free Presbyterian Church be the continuance of the Reformation Church when it seems to have reached a peak of perfection which Reformation Church denied was possible? How can it represent the Reformation Church when it will not allow any charge be brought against it though the vows expressly call office-bearers to exercise such a liberty?   These views represent the principles and practice of the moderates, not of the Evangelical stream which runs on from the Reformation, through the Disruption and through the action of Mr Macfarlane in 1893. The model and the reality do not add up.

So far as the present Free Church is concerned, I am taking to do with the historical past, though it projects its shadow into the present.   The Free Church has consistently accused the Free Presbyterian Church of schism, that is, of dropping out of the battle prematurely, like the sons of Ephraim of Ps. 78 who turned back in the day of battle.   The statement of February, 1893 which became the manifesto of the Constitutional Party from that time on, still finds them at that date confronting the enemy, as David fearlessly confronted Goliath.   It is a challenging model.   Their aim is to force the majority which by that time had passed the Declaratory Act to admit that the Act was not really law.   Yet all the time, I have argued, they were administering the Declaratory Act on the terms of the majority.   The model may be that of a free and courageous David in uncompromising conflict with the enemies of the Lord.   The reality is rather of a bound Samson forced to comply with the will of the Philistines.

Finally, it seems to me very sad that after a century the three Churches which came from the break-up of the Free Church are still dancing to the tune set by the leaders in the Old Free Church. Why did Dr Rainy not pass the Declaratory Act in 1892 as a package; why did he not make an admission from the outset that the Declaratory Act was binding on all as a bond of union, and not put in the preamble that it was for the relief only of some; why not have the Questions and Formula changed at the same 1892 Assembly, so that the Assembly could have been spared the vain talk of the possibility of a further stand being made some time down the line when the Questions and Formula were eventually changed; why receive protests in 1892 and refuse them in 1893? All this speaks to me of the intention of bending before the main brunt of the opposition in 1892 when protests were received, together with "stringing along" the protesters with hopes of further concessions. By the time that it was realised that these concessions were worthless, (1894), the energy of protest had been sapped, and it was at any rate clear that with the removal of protests in 1893, no effective opposition could any more be given.

Doubtless, the aim of such a strategy was to keep the ranks of the Free Church intact. The experiment did not work. Had it been made clear that the constitution was changed in 1892, there would have been a mass exodus in that year of the whole Constitutional Party. There would have been one instead of three churches today in the Highlands adhering to the Westminster Confession. Instead of this we have the Free Presbyterian Church representing the stance of a church which separated in 1892. We have the APC representing a church which adopts, (according to my view), the views of Mr Macfarlane who separated in 1893. Finally, we have the Free Church which did not separate at all at that time, and waited till the actual union of United Presbyterian Church and Free Church in 1900, though they admitted in the law-case of 1904 a change had been made in the Constitution by the Declaratory Act by the Declaratory Act.

What we are doing now is defining our relative identities according to an agenda set, not by ourselves, but by the Church from which we all separated. The Free Presbyterian Church says the Free Church compromised truth in staying in the Declaratory

Act Free Church beyond 1893. The Free Church says the Free Presbyterian Church was schismatic in separating prematurely. Is it not time there was an open examination of the roots of the relative separations without consideration of where this might lead in relation to property? At present the three churches have an image rather closer than comfort to the caricature of the old Highland clans - strong in a hearty loyalty to nearest and dearest, and to the causes which their respective traditions dictated, while weak in an independent and objective examination of the real nature of the loyalty which bound them, and the differences which separated them from their opponents, and weak in a realistic assessment of the final outcome.

Our principal enemy is not found within any circle that might be drawn round the three churches. It is without, in the prevailing godlessness of our communities. Just this morning, (26th Dec. '95), I heard the words on the radio, "There is no Jesus, there are no laws written on tablets of stone. Everything is relative." It is that enemy which is bringing paganism into our schools, the values by which our social policies are determined, and into the government of the nation as a whole. It is against that enemy our main energies should be directed. That, in turn, can only happen in complete unity of spirit when the differences that divide us have been honestly faced up to and assessed for what they are, if not totally resolved.

"With men, this is impossible, but with God, all things are possible," (Matt. 19;26).

NOTE ON PROTESTS AGAINST ASSEMBLIES.

In Pt. 2, ch2, it was said that protest against the supreme authority, as against protest against the act of a supreme authority, brought separation. There are at least two cases early in Scottish Reformation history when protest against the supreme authority did not, indeed, bring separation. In 1618 there was a protest against the Assembly which passed the five articles of Perth as "neither free, nor full, nor formal" (Calderwood, VII, p. 428). In 1651 there was a protest against the Assembly that passed the Resolutions about how "malignants" were to be dealt with. In neither case was there separation, though after 1651, rival presbyteries were set up.

The reason in the first case was partly that the Five Articles of Perth were not rigidly enforced, (Donaldson, "Scottish Church History" pp. 208-211), and partly that the protesters took a spiritual view of the Church. "We have cause to weep for our harlot-mother; her Husband (Christ) is sending her to Rome's brothel house...Yet...this Church shall sing the bridegroom's welcome home again to His own house." (Rutherford, Letters, vol. ii, 50.). Rutherford views himself as connected with the Church not, perhaps, directly, (he was dismissed by his bishop and banished to Aberdeen in 1636), but through Christ the head of the Church. Hence he did not separate. The same was doubtless true of the protest in 1651, in which Rutherford took a prominent part. Are lessons to be learnt here?

A somewhat similar situation took place in 1893. Mr Macfarlane did, indeed, take up a separate position within the Free Church with his protest against the 1893 Assembly, but he did not immediately separate. If, as he says in his Kishorn lecture, Christ in the court of heaven decided in favour of the 1892 protesters, then he had a right to remain with the congregation in Raasay, claim the manses and churches of the Free Church as rightly his, preside at the next communion, and take others into association with his own position in Millhouse and at Raasay itself. All these he did. One thing he would not do was associate himself with his brethren in the presbytery. It was the presbytery which would implement the Declaratory Act.

Dr Rainy had promised a committee to look into Mr Macfarlane's protest. It must have been evident to Mr Macfarlane, however, that the Free Church authorities would not long brook his conduct, however he might be able to justify himself to himself. Before proceedings were taken against him he broke the tension by drawing up his Reasons of Separation in August 1893 and inaugurating the first presbytery of the Free Presbyterian Church.

ABERTARFF FREE CHURCH PRESBYTERY, JAN. 17, 1893.
ENTRY OF PROTEST INTO PRESBYTERY RECORDS.

SPEECH OF MR MACFARLANE REPORTED IN "THE NORTHERN CHRONICLE", JAN. 25TH, 1893

"..... He felt bound, not only by his ordination vows, but as a professing Christian, to use every legitimate means to oppose this Declaratory Act, forced upon them by the General Assembly. He did not believe that the Act would ever be rescinded, and one effect of it would be that they would have another disruption in the Free Church - ('No, no, never' from several of the members). It would be sad that they should have in 1893 a disruption as they had in 1843, (Mr Sutherland, 'Nonsense'). He did not know what to say to the conscience of ministers who had travelled long distances to make speeches against this same Act, and now refused to support the protests. He had much pleasure in seconding the motion."

REASONS OF DISSENT AND APPEAL to the SYNOD OF GLENELG, against the Resolution of the Presbytery of Abertarff of 17th January, 1893, to record in their minutes a Protest against the action of the Assembly in 1892, in passing the Declaratory Act into a Standing Law of the Church, and **ANSWERS of the Presbytery.**

1. The Resolution appealed against being a Protest by an Inferior Court against an Act of the Supreme Court of the Church, it is ultra vires of the Presbytery to record it in their minutes.

    Answer: It is admitted that in the ordinary administration of the Laws of the Church it is ultra vires of an Inferior Court to disobey the orders of a Superior; but the constitution of the Church being mutually agreed upon by all her office-bearers, it is now ultra vires of the majority to put their own and a different construction upon that constitution, as is done by the Declaratory Act.

2. The Protest is, in effect, a Resolution by the Presbytery to disobey an Act of the Supreme Court of the Church, which Protest is illegal and subversive of discipline.

Answer: If this reason is valid, the Declaratory Act must be believed and adopted by every individual office-bearer in this Church, whereas the Act, itself, states, and its introducers explain, its object is to relieve the scruples of those who entertain them; this Presbytery, entertaining no such scruples regarding any of the doctrines of the Confession, are at liberty to reject and protest against said Act, for they cannot conceive how, as individuals, they are at liberty to reject it, but that the Presbytery is bound to submit to it.

3. Such a Protest is useless to accomplish any practical purpose, and the only effective remedy by any Court of the Church disapproving of an Act of Assembly is to overture the General Assembly to amend or repeal the Act disapproved of; and other reasons to be stated at the bar.

Answer: The Presbytery look upon this Protest for the purpose of resisting the Declaratory Act far more hopeful and useful than overturing the Assembly for its repeal; for no-one believes the Assembly shall do so, while the protest secures us against compliance with the said Act, and is a bond of union among those who mean to resist it.

Mr Macfarlane was one of two who defended the action of the Presbytery at the bar of the Synod.

REV. DONALD MACFARLANE'S PROTEST, 1893.

Whereas by the action of the General Assembly of 1892 in passing the Declaratory Act into a law of the Church, and by that Act being retained in her constitution, the Church, in our opinion, ceases to be the true representative of the Free Church of Scotland; and whereas by our ordination vows, we are bound by the most solemn obligations to assert, maintain and defend the doctrines and constitution of the said Church, and to follow no divisive courses from the doctrine, worship, discipline, government and exclusive jurisdiction of the same, I, the undersigned minister of the Free Church, in my own name and in the name of all who may adhere to me, declare that, whatever I may subsequently do, neither my conscience nor my ordination vows allow me to act under what has now been made law in this Church.

I also protest against the despotic power exercised by a majority of the office-bearers of this Church in making changes in her creed and constitution, which are ultra vires of any majority in the face of any protesting minority, and I declare that I claim my sacred and civil rights according to the terms of contract agreed upon between me and the Free Church at my ordination, and in accordance with the creed and constitution of the Free Church in the year 1843.

I have not included the Free Church Declaratory Act, itself, among the Appendices. The text is available either in Free Church histories like that of Dr. Stewart and Prof. Cameron or in the Free Presbyterian Church History. The doctrinal changes brought in by the Act are not the main concern of this book, but rather the various responses to the Act.

THE DECLARATORY ACT IN COURT

Memoir of Rev. D. Macfarlane

(p. 147) "A disagreement arose between two parties concerning important matters in the Christian religion. The name of one was D.A., a mere stripling and self-conceited, as the young in years are naturally prone to be. The name of the other was C.F., an old party of long experience, of mature judgment, and highly respected by experienced and well-grounded followers in the doctrines and practices of the faith as clearly set forth in the Word of God. .... The case of contention between them was repeatedly tried in the Courts of the Church, and at length decided in favour of the younger party - like the case of Rehoboam, (2 Chron. x), who followed the advice of the young instead of the old men, and brought judgments on the nation. The young party had many followers in a back-sliding age, but the old party protested and appealed to a higher court - the Court of heaven - to finally decide the case; as there was no higher court to appeal to.

God was the Judge, speaking through His Word, and it was the standard by which the case was tried and finally settled. The court-house was filled with anxious listeners, among whom were many ministers and office-bearers, who were self confident that the case would be settled in favour of D.A., as it had been in the lower courts. But the case was not to be settled or decided this time by majorities, but by the Judge who is just in all His ways and holy in all His works. He would decide the case impartially in favour of the one who had truth on his side.

p. 160 "The huge audience were now anxiously awaiting to hear what the Judge had to say in summing up the case.

p. 161 " 'I approve of every statement in C.F.'s document, as all statements therein are supported by my Word of truth, and I, as Judge of all, through my Word, condemn D.A. and acquit C.F. from the charge brought against him by his accuser; but as I am a long-suffering God, and delight in mercy, while judgment is my strange work, I will give D.A.'s followers an opportunity of renouncing their errors and of returning to sound doctrine, but if not, their blood shall be on their own head.'

"The Judge, in addressing D.A. asked him what he was to do. D.A. refused to retract any of his statements, holding that, according to his opinion, he did not forsake the truth. The Judge - 'Do you think yourself wiser than I? If so, you must bear the consequences of your disobedience, and also all your followers.'

"There was great commotion over the decision of the Judge. Those who adhered to C.F. protested against the arrogant manner in which D.A. tried to compel all to accept his views, and by their protest and determined adherence to C.F. made a faithful stand according to the grace given to them for the original standards of faith and practice held by the fathers in 1843, their eyes looking unto the hills from whence cometh their help, even to him who made heaven and earth, trusting that he would sustain them in providence, as well as in grace - yea, looking to Him who saith - 'Be thou faithful unto death and I will give thee a crown of life.' "

THE FREE CHURCH OF SCOTLAND, 1843-1910, by Rev. A. Stewart and Rev. Prof. J. Kennedy Cameron.

This book remains the main history on the side of the Free Church covering the period of the separation of both Free Church and Free Presbyterian Churches. It has been re-issued in recent times.

In dealing with the relative positions of the Free Presbyterian Church and Free Church it is defective in a number of ways.

1. The true position in relation to the formula is nowhere set out and cannot be deduced by the reader since the full wording of the formula is not given. The writers say, (p. 76), "They (those who were being ordained) still declared their belief in 'the whole doctrine of the Confession of Faith'; they still expressed their conviction that 'the doctrine therein contained is the true doctrine.' "   Were the full text given, it would be clear that another meaning can be taken from the words, as has already been pointed out previously.   "Whole doctrine" could be linked equally well with "approven by former General Assemblies of this Church". In this case men might freely avail themselves of the Declaratory Act. Lord Trayner, in comparing the respective formulae of the Free Church and the United Free Church says in the Court of Session, "If any change is introduced it must be one 'approven' by the principal judicatory of the Church, and in regard to this the formulae do not differ." In his view there is no doubt about the linking of "whole doctrine" with 'approven', nor that the bringing in of a new formula   leaving out the word, "whole",   would   make   no   effective   difference   to   the implementation of the Act. (The proposed Formula which was

dropped would have omitted the word, "whole", as did the United Free Church Formula in 1900).

2. The impression is given that the 1894 Declaratory Act was brought in because of the disturbance in the Highlands following the secession of 1893, (p.73). It could be gathered from this that the Constitutional Party post-1893 had a kind of protection not afforded to those who separated. This act was, in fact, planned from the outset. "The Committee came to be of the opinion that it was not necessary to introduce any reference to the Declaratory Act into the Questions nor into the Formula, but that the purposes contemplated by the Church could be best secured by a Declaration in the Preamble of the Act which may be passed to authorise the revised questions. The declaration proposed is as follows: 'While the Church does not impose upon her office-bearers acceptance of the statements in the Declaratory Act, 1892, anent the Confession of Faith, all who answer the Questions and sign the Formula herewith enacted are entitled to do so in view of that Declaratory Act.' Such a declaration, it appeared to the Committee, will adequately guard against laying any new burden on entrants, while it makes clear the right of those who desire it to benefit by the measure of relief afforded in the Declaratory Act." (1892 Report of the Committee on the Confession of Faith).

The 1894 Declaratory Act , of which the above was an embryonic form, was, in fact, to be brought in in parallel with the changes in the Questions and Formula. The fact that it was still brought in, and hence men werfe entitled to sign the Formula in view of the Declaratory Act, in spite of the dropping of these changes, demonstrates that the changes were not needed to bring the (1892) Declaratory Act into operation.

3. The key question is never addressed in the book as to whether the contract of association was changed by the introduction of the Declaratory Act. The passing of the (1894) Declaratory Act

shows quite clearly that it was, and that the contract had been changed from the outset, since the 1894 Act simply verified what had been the case for the preceding two years. The real question was not whether men were free to preach the whole length and breadth of the doctrine of the Westminster Confession or not, but whether they were part of an association in which others were not so bound. Prior to 1892, all were united in belief in the common standard of the Confession of Faith. From that date onward, men were claiming the right to take their vows "in view of the Declaratory Act", and had no protection been available, the Constitutional Party, whatever their personal beliefs and their freedom to express these beliefs, would have been bound in association with them.

4. The relation of the Constitutional Party to the protest of 1892 is not even touched upon. The only real defence after 1892 for the Constitutional Party was to protest that the Act would not be binding on them in any shape or form. This they did. The June 1892 Convention decided to fight on under the shelter of a protest. All other aspects of the armoury of the Constitutional Party, protests before entering into discussion, overtures for the repeal of the Act, dissents when they did not get their way are emphasised, but this vital means of opposing the Act in 1892 does not rate even a bare mention. There is a mention of the protest of Mr Macfarlane in 1893, but not that the protest of Mr Macfarlane was a protest against the despotic power which brought in changes ultra vires of the protesting minority. The only reason I can think why there should be this total silence is that mention of the protest would highlight the apparent change in policy when it was claimed in February, 1893, that sufficient protection was to be found in the fact that the Questions and Formula were not changed. The protection of the protest then became redundant.